Published By:

VANDANA PUBLICATIONS

VARANASI, U.P.

New Edition :2018-19

Rev. Edition :2019-20

© COPYRIGHT WITH THE AUTHORS ONLY.

(No part of the book can be reprinted without permission of the Authors)

PRICE: Rs 250/-

NTA NET COMMERCE FOUNDATION

1000 MCQ SERIES–

MARKETING MANAGMENT

1. All marketing activities revolves around –

   1. Exchange process
   2. Selling process
   3. Purchase process
   4. Production process

2. Match the following

List – I (Functions of Marketing Process) (Area)	List – II
1. Functions of Exchange	(i) Selling
2. Transfer of Ownership	(ii) Buying and Selling
3. Functions of Transportations	(iii)
4. Facilitating Functions	(iv) Financing
	(v) Costing

Codes :

	(a)	(b)	(c)	(d)
1.	1	2	3	4
2.	4	2	3	1
3.	3	1	2	4
4.	2	3	1	4

3. **Match the following**

List – I	List – II
(P's of Marketing)	(Elements)

1.	Product	(i)	Warranty
2.	Price Facility	(ii)	Credit
3.	Promotion Selling	(iii)	Personal
4.	Place Location (Distribution)	(iv)	Factory
		(v)	Marketing

Codes :

	(a)	(b)	(c)	(d)
1.	1	2	3	4
2.	4	3	2	1
3.	3	1	2	4
4.	2	1	3	4

4. **Match the following**

List – I	List – II

(Bases of Segmenting Industrial Market)		(Factors)	
1.	Physical Industry	(i)	Size of
2.	Operational Policy	(ii)	Logistic
3.	Purchases	(iii)	Lobby Status
4.	Situational Order	(iv)	Specific
		(v)	Risk Factor

Codes :

	(a)	(b)	(c)	(d)
1.	1	2	3	4
2.	4	5	1	2
3.	2	3	1	4
4.	4	5	1	2

5. Match the following

List – I		List – II	
(Marketing Sub-plans)		(Factors)	
1.	Base Line	(i)	Market
2.	Research	(ii)	Segmentation
3.	Technical Plan	(iii)	Branding
4.	Organizational Plan	(iv)	Distribution
5.	Contingency Plan Expansion	(v)	Market
		(vi)	Tax

Codes :

	(a)	(b)	(c)	(d)
1.	2	3	4	1
2.	**1**	**2**	**3**	**4**
3.	1	3	2	4
4.	1	2	4	3

6. Match the following

List – I		List – II	
(Marketing Sub-plans)		**(Variables)**	
1.	Baseline Research Service	(i)	Customer
2.	Technical Plan	(ii)	Packaging
3.	Organisational Plan	(iii)	Regulation
4.	Contingency Plan Management	(iv)	Risk
		(v)	Tax

Codes :

	(a)	(b)	(c)	(d)
1.	**1**	**2**	**3**	**4**
2.	2	3	1	4
3.	1	3	2	4
4.	4	2	3	1

7. Match the following

List – I		List – II	
(Authors)		**(Ideas)**	
1.	Bill Bishop Marketing for the Digital Age	(i)	Strategic

2.	D Bird	(ii)	Commonsense Direct Marketing
3.	Daniel S. Jonal	(iii)	Online Marketing
4.	Jeffery F. Rayport	(iv)	Managing is the Market space
		(v)	e-commerce

Codes :

	(a)	(b)	(c)	(d)
1.	1	2	3	4
2.	5	1	4	3
3.	3	1	2	4
4.	3	2	4	1

8. Match the following

List – I		List – II	
(Product on the Basis of Psychology)		**(Examples)**	
1.	Pestige Products	(i)	Ownership on the Car
2.	Maturity Products	(ii)	Cold drink
3.	Anxiety Products	(iii)	Swap
4.	Hedonic Products	(iv)	Biscuit and Bread
		(v)	Firm

Codes :

	(a)	(b)	(c)	(d)
1.	1	2	3	4
2.	4	3	1	2
3.	1	2	4	3

4.   2   1   3   4

9. If market research shows that aggregate of people do not desire a particular product, the people in that aggregate;

a. Are a market for the product
b. Do not have the ability to purchase the product
c. **Are not a market for the product**
d. Are a market but will not purchase the product.

10. Which of the following is an example of a customer in an organizational market?

a. A homemaker who buys detergent
b. A customer who hires a solicitor
c. A shop owner who buys pencils for use in his shop
d. **A plant manager who buys petrol for his car**

11..The two approaches to identify a target market are;

a. Total market and undifferentiated approaches
b. Product differentiation and customer differentiation approaches
c. Multisegment and concentration approach
d. **Total market and market segmentation approach**

12.Statement(I): Designing a distribution system for a service (for-profit or non-business context) involves to select the parties only through which ownership will pass.
      Statement(II):   The ownership channel for most of the services is long and quite complex because of inseparability characteristic.

Statement(III): Short channel susually mean more control on the part of the seller.

Identify the correct code of being the statements correct or incorrect. These statements relate to channel strategies of products /services.

a. Statements (I) and (II) are correct but (III) is not correct.
b. Statements (I) and (III)are correct but (II) is not correct.
c. **Statements (I) and (II) are not correct but (III) is correct.**
d. Statements (I),(II) and (III) all are not correct.

13. An enormous collection of data on various topics from a variety of internal and external sources, compiled by a firm for its own use or for use by its clients, is called:

    a. Data-base   b. Data warehouse

    c. Data mining   d. M.I.S.

14. Decision making involves the choice of a course of action is –

    1. Achieve success
    2. Achieve sale Target
    3. **Achieve pre Determined objectives**
    4. Achieve incentive targets

15. A decision is generally express as

    1. A policy
    2. A case
    3. **A motive**
    4. A directive

16. Which of the following is a part of incidents ?

    1. Present incident
    2. Past incident
    3. Future incident
    4. **1, 2 and 3**

17. Different decisions are –

    1. Inter related
    2. Inter dependent
    3. Outer
    4. **1 & 2**

18. Decision making is a process of –

    1. Dispersion
    2. Discrete
    3. **Continuity**
    4. Observation

19. Which of the following describes the nature of Decision Making?

    1. Process of continuity
    2. Commitment
    3. Evaluation
    4. Birth to new decisions
    5. **All of above**

20. A decision reflects –

    1. Media
    2. Method of solving problem
    3. **Commitment of decision maker**
    4. Enterprise's Growth
    5. Care by owner

21. All the business activities are performed in accordance with the decisions taken by the –

    1. Lower level management
    2. Top level management
    3. Middle level management
    4. Junior level management
    5. Senior level management

22. In the process of decision making the available resources / alternatives are –

    1. Analysed
    2. Observed
    3. Compared
    4. All of above
    5. None of above

23. Which aspect of decision making put more emphasis on the need of proper Environment ?

    1. Proper environment
    2. Environment of decision making
    3. Time of decision
    4. Psychological factor
    5. Employees participation

24. If there is only one method / way of doing a particular act, there is no need of –

    1. Management
    2. Need of decision taking
    3. Need of trading
    4. Need of environment
    5. Need of process

25. What will happen if the decisions are not implemented ?

    1.   Wastage of time
    2.   Wastage of money
    3.   Wastage of entertainment
    4.   Wastage of all resources
    5.   **1, 2 and 4**

26. Which aspect of the nature of decision making emphasise on having proper time of decision making ?

    1.   Time lapse
    2.   Speed
    3.   **Time of decision making**
    4.   Quality time
    5.   Quality of time

27. If the decisions are not taken at its proper time, it will cause various problem for –

    1.   Top level management
    2.   Middle level management
    3.   Lower level management
    4.   Outer level management
    5.   **All of the above**

28. The decision maker should have which of the following qualities ?

    1.   Ability
    2.   Fatness
    3.   Intelligence
    4.   Experience
    5.   **1, 3 and 4**

29. The factor which should be taken care of at the time of decision taking is

1. Social environment
2. Linking
3. Disliking
4. Political learnings
5. **All of above**

30. Whose participation is most required in the process of decision making ?

1. Middle level management
2. Sources
3. **Subordinates**
4. Top level management
5. None of above

31. Which aspect of decision making emphasis on contribution from subordinates ?

1. Participation
2. **Participation of employee**
3. Participation of government
4. Participation of competitors
5. Participation of consumers

32. Decisions and its communication must go –

1. Separately
2. **Together**
3. One by one
4. Depends on situation
5. As per nature

33. implementation of decision can be ensured only when these are ………. Communicated.

1. Timely
2. Clearly
3. Combinally

    4. Properly
    5. **1, 2 and 4**

34. Marketing decisions defines the

    1. Scope of marketing activities
    2. Duties
    3. Responsibilities
    4. Power of employees
    5. **All of above**

35. Marketing decisions are very critical because –

    1. Achievement of marketing objective
    2. Success of enterprise depends on it
    3. Purchase depends on it
    4. All the activities depends on it
    5. **1 and 2**

36. Which of the following is one of the types of decisions ?

    1. Major
    2. Minor
    3. Routine
    4. Rare
    5. **All of above**

37. Marketing discovers the –

    1. Needs of consumer
    2. Wants of consumer
    3. Needs of Government
    4. Needs of tax authorities
    5. **1 and 2**

38. How marketing effects the demand ?

1.	Create demand of product
2.	Create demand of existing product
3.	Maintain demand of new product
4.	1 and 3
5.	**1, 2 and 3**

39 Decrease in distribution cost directly effects the –

1. **Price of product**
2. Quality of product
3. Quantity of product
4. All of above
5. None of above

40. There are successful operation of marketing activities in employment opportunities because –

1. **Expansion needs more man power**
2. Expansion needs more machine
3. Expansion needs more product
4. Expansion needs more space
5. Expansion needs more technique

41. Which is one of the activities involved in marketing ?

1. Transport
2. Communication
3. Storage
4. Warehousing etc
5. **All of above**

42. Successful operation of marketing activities is to increase the sales, thus it helps in increasing-

1. **National income**
2. Sale price
3. Purchase price
4. Cost of products

5. Distribution cost

43. Marketing research reduces overall cost and helps in increasing –

    1. **Profits**
    2. Other costs
    3. Nominal cost
    4. Competition

44. Which is the most important activity in any business concern ?

    1. Employees
    2. Purchase
    3. Government
    4. **Marketing**
    5. Schedule

45. Name the inversely accepted business activity which is required for all the successful business ?

    1. Production
    2. Marketing
    3. Purchase
    4. Schedule
    5. Raw material

46. The firm should decide what can be sold before deciding –

    1. Marketing
    2. Production
    3. What can be produced
    4. Channel of distribution
    5. None of these

47. Who said "Product is a cluster of psychological satisfactions" ?

    1. **George Fisk**
    2. Prof. Diya Parashar
    3. Dr. Manmohan Singh
    4. Rustom S. Davar
    5. Dr. Pankaj Parashar

48. What is a product ?

    1. Goods which are produced for the sale purpose of consumption
    2. **Anything that satisfies consumers wants or needs and involves transfer of title**
    3. Anything that satisfies a need or want and can be offered on the market for attention, acquisition use or consumption, including physical objects, services, organizations ideas and mixes of the above
    4. Any physical good
    5. Goods that satisfy a want or need and that consumers can actually see or touch

49. The three levels of product are –

    1. Raw, Semi finished & finished
    2. **Core product, Actual product and Augmented promotion**
    3. Price, place, Promotion
    4. Design, Brand, Name and Packaging
    5. Tangible Product, Services ideas

50. Product planners must think of products and services on three levels.

   1. **True**
   2. True when choices are limited
   3. True in case of Multilevel product
   4. False
   5. False when products is of durable nature

51. The following represents perhaps the most distinctive skill of professional marketers as they create, maintain, protect and enhance consumer perception of a product or service. What is it?

   1. Trade mark
   2. Design of a striking symbol
   3. Personal sales
   4. **Branding**
   5. Performance

52. A brand serves to identify the maker or seller of a product and may consist of –

   1. **A name, term, sign, symbol, design**
   2. A board
   3. A catchy slogan
   4. A powerful name
   5. A high price tag

53. Major branding decisions include brand name selection, brand sponsor and strategy

1. **True**
2. True when brand is so famous
3. True when brand is very simple
4. False
5. False in some special cases

54. If a protected brand name becomes too successful, a company can lose the exclusive rights to that name :

1. False if found guilty
2. False
3. False in somecases
4. **True**
5. True when brand is not so tipicle

55. A company has four choices when it comes to brand strategy, new brands, multi brands …… & ……. .

1. Pure and impure
2. Line extension and line creation
3. **Line extension and brand extension**
4. Brand extension and brand creation
5. Line creation and brand creation

56. Making a major product line decision involves determining

1. **Product line length**
2. Product line stretching
3. The marketing mix
4. Classification
5. Diversification

57. Which of the following is not a step in the new product development process ?

   1. Marketing
   2. Test marketing
   3. Concept development and testing
   4. Market research

58. New to the word products where the category itself is new, are also known as –

   1. Specialty products
   2. Diffusions
   3. Innovations
   4. Inventions

59. Product is the .... of all the marketing activities.

   1. Bottom
   2. Top
   3. Centre
   4. Source

60. Two most important variables of marketing is

   1. Consumer
   2. Wholeseller
   3. Product
   4. 1 and 3

61. A change in the minimum drinking age in India presents a change in which of the following   for Bass Brewery ?

   1. Marketing mix
   2. Marketing environment
   3. Marketing concept
   4. None of these

62. If MK invest was to perceive that consumers within a particular group were becoming more conservative in their investing, and thus developed more products with lower risk, it would be :

    1. **Responding to the marketing environment**
    2. Changing its target market
    3. Developing a sales orientation
    4. Changing its organization structure

63. Capri is a brand of cigarette that contains low tar and slim in design to appeal to women. In this instance, women comprise Capri's :

    1. Marketing mix
    2. **Target market**
    3. Target audience
    4. Marketing strategy

64. When Dupont develops new carpets that are highly stain resistant and durable, it must educate consumers about the product's benefits. This calls for activity in which of the following marketing mix variables ?

    1. Price
    2. **Promotion**
    3. Distribution
    4. Product

65. Why are marketers interested in the level of disposable income ?

    1. It accurately represents future buying power
    2. It increase current buying power
    3. It is what is left after taxes to buy luxuries with
    4. **It is a ready source of buying power**

66. Which of the following companies would probably be most interested in tracking discretionary income levels ?

   1. Asda supermarkets
   2. **BMW automobiles**
   3. The post office
   4. Kraft general foods

67. What type of competitive structure exists when a firm produces a product that has no close substitutes ?

   1. **Monopoly**
   2. Oligopoly
   3. Monopolistic competition
   4. Perfect competition

68. In the beer industry, a few large brewers supply the majority of the market. The brewing industry is an example of which of the following competitive structures ?

   1. Monopoly
   2. **Oligopoly**
   3. Monopolistic competition
   4. Perfect competition
   5. None of these

69. Which of the following firms would most likely have a monopoly for its competitive environment ?

   1. **Sunset cablevision**
   2. Montgomery transport
   3. Post office parcel services
   4. Telecom car phones

5. None of these

70. Essex office products has decided to use a particular competitive tool that it feels will have a major impact. Its consultant. Dr. Bell, contends that this particular approach is the one most easily copied by the firm's competitors. The tool in question is :

    1. Price
    2. Market segmentation
    3. Distribution
    4. Promotion
    5. None of these

71. A small hardware store whose only competitor is a huge discount store would be least likely to use which competitive tool ?

    1. Service
    2. Price
    3. Product offering
    4. Distribution

72. Technology assessment is :

    1. Assessing how much technology has been incorporated into an organization
    2. Trying to foresee the effects of new products and processes on a firm's operation and on society in general
    3. Assessing how much technology one wants to put into a company in the future
    4. Assessing the cost of new whether a firm can afford to use it

73. When Bell Laboratories attempts to anticipate the effect of new products and processes on its own innovations, other business organizations, and society in general, it is engaging in :

    1. Product differentiation
    2. Monopolistic competition
    3. Technology assessment
    4. Innovative marketing

74. If VIDEOCON developed a new technology that made 3-D imagery possible through the use of videotape played on an advanced television set, it would be more likely to market this innovation if it could obtain a :

    1. Competitive advancement
    2. Patent
    3. Low price advantage
    4. Technological assessment

75. Which of the following represents an output from the marketing environment ?

    1. Money borrowed by Liverpool F.C. to help finance its operations
    2. Nike's television advertising compaign featuring a leading sports personality
    3. Information on shoppers' attitudes purchased by Debenhams Department stores
    4. Steel purchased by Volvo to be used in producing cars

76. Compaq computers collects information about political, legal, regulatory, societal, economic, competitive and technological forces that may affect its marketing activities. This process is called :

    1. environmental scanning
    2. Survey of environment
    3. Marketing information analysis
    4. Environmental analysis

77. When pepsi Co takes the information collected through research and attempts to assess and interpret what it means for its soft drink marketing efforts, pepsi Co is involved in environmental :

    1. Scanning
    2. Forces
    3. Management
    4. Analysis

78. After Compaq computer gathers information related to its marketing environment, it attempts to define current environmental changes, allowing it to determine possible opportunities and threats facing the company this process is called :

    1. Environmental scanning
    2. Survey of environment
    3. Marketing planning
    4. Environmental analysis

79. If cigarette manufacturers were to lobby parliament to get restrictions on cigarette advertising eased, their environmental response would best be described as :

    1. Passive
    2. Reactive
    3. Proactive
    4. Conservative

80. There are two major categories of laws that directly affect marketing practices: precompetitive legislation and :

    1. Consumer protection legislation
    2. Unfair trade practices laws
    3. Trading standards legislation
    4. Consumer price discrimination legislation

81. If the national Association of Hoisery Manufactures sets guidelines for its member firms to follow regarding the use of unethical practices, it is engaging in :

    1. Legislation
    2. Lobbying
    3. Self-regulation
    4. Environmental scanning

82. The consumer movement is :

    1. Against foreign imports that are much cheaper than products produced in the home market
    2. A movement that is trying to improve consumer satisfaction
    3. A social movement that is able to challenge big business practices
    4. A diverse group of individuals, groups and organizations attempting to protect the rights of consumers

83. Lynx has demonstrated against the sale of coats made of animal furs. This group's efforts to change shoppers' attitudes represents .... for fur retailers.

    1. An opportunity
    2. Self regulation
    3. A social force
    4. An economic force

84. The period in the business cycle in which there is extremely high unemployment, low wages, minimum total disposable income and a lack of confidence in the economy by consumers is :

    1. Recovery
    2. Prosperity
    3. Depression

4. Recession

85. Global marketing is

   1. **The development of marketing strategies for the entire world or major regions of the world**
   2. Performing marketing activities across national boundaries
   3. The creation of value and the exchange of value between countries
   4. Having firms with operations or subsidiaries located in many countries

86. The Chairman of Unilever states that the world is just one big market. He feels is just anyone not taking this stance is systematically passing up profitable business. His approach MOST closely resembles

   1. Exporting
   2. **Global marketing**
   3. Export marketing
   4. Full scale international marketing

87. McDonald's and KFC satisfy hungry consumers in every hemisphere. This is an example of

   1. **Globalization**
   2. Customization
   3. Internationalization
   4. Regionalization

88. Which of the following is not limited service wholesalers ?

   1. Distributors
   2. Cash wholesalers
   3. **Industrial distributors**
   4. Rack Jobbers

89. Transporters wholesalers, drop shippers are examples of full services wholesalers.

    1. True
    2. False
    3. True when wholesalers has all India presence
    4. True in special conditions

90. Which of the following results from vertical integration by sellers or buyers ?

    1. Brokers
    2. Merchant wholesalers
    3. Manufactures's sales branches and offices
    4. Rack Jobbers's

91. Which of the following is not a future retailing trend ?

    1. Rise in competitions
    2. The rise of mega retailers
    3. The global expansion of major retailers
    4. The trend to limit the type of goods sold through each type of retail store

92. Main type of Buyers in Super Bazar are

    1. Higher income class
    2. Lower income class
    3. Middle income class
    4. People from all the category

93. What is the sale technique of departmental stores ?

    1. Sales by salesman
    2. Based on self service
    3. As per a management
    4. As and where basis

94. What is the nature of sale in departmental stores ?

   1. Credit
   2. Cash and credit both
   3. Only credit
   4. Only cash

95. What is the basis of difference among departmental stores and multiple shops ?

   1. Nature of product
   2. Price of product
   3. Credit facilities
   4. All of above

96. At which place one can find all type of products ?

   1. Multiple shops
   2. Wholesalers
   3. Ration shops
   4. Departmental stores

97. Shops selling the products of only one manufacture are called

   1. Departmental store
   2. Multiple shops
   3. Wholesale trade
   4. Ration shops

98. Which rank a Wholesalers holds in Mediator channel ?

   1. First
   2. Second
   3. Third
   4. Fifth

99. Which rank a Retailer holds in Mediator channel ?

1. First
2. Third
3. Second
4. Last

100. Amount of risk in wholesale is

    1. Less
    2. Average
    3. More
    4. Normal

101. Two concepts of product are

    1. Narrow concept
    2. Line concept
    3. Wide concept
    4. 1 and 3

102. "A product is a bundle of physical or chemical properties" states .... concept of product.

    1. Tall
    2. Narrow
    3. Wide
    4. Straight

103. What is one of the examples of narrow concept ?

    1. Soap
    2. Fan
    3. Table
    4. Chair
    5. All of above

104. "Product means all the goods and services which may satisfy the needs and wants of customers" states …….. concepts of product.

    1. Table
    2. Chair
    3. **Same shampoo available in 5 different packings**
    4. Mouth freshener

105. If the first commandant in marketing is known as the customer, the second is ……….. .

    1. **Product**
    2. Raw material
    3. Finished material
    4. Useless material
    5. Safe material

106. All the marketing efforts …… and ……... with product.

    1. **Starts and End**
    2. Begin and Mid
    3. Save and Secure
    4. Long and Short
    5. Brave and Safe

107. What is the main classification of products ?

    1. Consumer product
    2. Industrial product
    3. Safe product
    4. Defence product
    5. **1, 2 and 4**

108. What the sub-division of consumer products ?

    1. Convenience
    2. Shopping
    3. Specially

4. **All of above**
5. None of these

109. Products which are made for direct consumption by the consumer are called –

1. Small product
2. Big product
3. **Consumer product**
4. Industrial product
5. None of these

110. Example of consumer products is

1. Scooter
2. Tyre
3. Book
4. **Pen**
5. All of above

111. The goods which are purchased by consumers very frequently are called :

1. Consumer Goods
2. **Convenience Goods**
3. Shopping Goods
4. Industrial Goods
5. Speciality Goods

112. Convenience Goods are ………. In nature.

1. Durable
2. Semi durable
3. **Non durable**
4. Perishable
5. None of above

113. The goods which are purchased by customers only after comparing their quality, price and other things are called ………. .

1. Convenience Goods
2. Shopping Goods
3. Speciality Goods
4. Normal Goods
5. Abnormal Goods

114. Example of shopping Goods is …………..

1. Furniture
2. Clothes
3. Shoes
4. Sarees
5. All of above

115. These type of goods are having some unique characteristics –

1. Speciality goods
2. Clothes
3. Normal goods
4. Shopping goods
5. Simple goods

116. If Erin Farm insurance saw a sudden increase in the number of farmers seeking flood insurance in Ireland due to major floods in Britain, the floods would be presenting the company with a marketing :

1. Opportunity
2. Strategy
3. Concept
4. Mix
5. None of these

117. Amount of risk in retail business is

 1. Less than wholesalers
 2. Equals to wholesale
 3. More than wholesalers
 4. Average
 5. None of above

118. Credit facilities in retail trade is

 1. More
 2. Less
 3. Minimum
 4. Less than wholesalers
 5. None of these

119. Credit facilities in wholesale trade is

 1. More
 2. Less
 3. Minimum
 4. Less than retail trade
 5. None of above

120. Degree of importance of business place in retail trade is

 1. Minimum
 2. More
 3. Average
 4. Not applicable
 5. None of above

121. Degree of importance of business place in wholesale trade is

 1. Minimum
 2. More
 3. Average
 4. Not applicable

5. All of above

122. Scope of business areas –

    1. Wide in wholesale
    2. Narrow in retail
    3. Unlimited in wholesale
    4. 1 and 2
    5. None of above

123. Services of wholesalers to manufactures is

    1. Distribution services
    2. Demand analysis
    3. Helps in large scale production
    4. Proceed towards lesses
    5. 1, 2 and 3

124. Services of wholesalers to retailers is

    1. Financial help
    2. Consultations
    3. Stability in prices
    4. Specialization
    5. All of above

125. What type of relationship is there between consumer and retailer ?

    1. Direct
    2. Indirect
    3. Marginal
    4. Vertical
    5. Straight

126. Which type of decisions are taken in regular course of action ?

    1. Major decision

2. Risky decision
3. Routine decision
4. Rare decision
5. Minor decision

127. Which type of decisions are of repeatative nature ?

1. Minor decision
2. Important decision
3. Risky decision
4. Routine decision
5. Rare decision

128. Which type of decisions affect the profitability of organization ?

1. Vital decision
2. Important decision
3. Minor decision
4. Rare decision
5. 1 or 2

129. Example of vital dicision is

1. Purchase of new plant
2. Develop the capacity of existing plant
3. Purchase of raw material
4. Packing of product
5. 1 and 2

130. Which type of decisions are not taken repeatatively and regularly ?

1. Rare decision
2. Minor decision
3. Major decision
4. Policy decision
5. Important decision

131. Example of rare decision is

    1. To change the channel of distribution
    2. To change the advertising agency
    3. To change organizational structure
    4. To change sales organization
    5. All of above

132. Which type of decision is made at different time intervals ?

    1. Recurring decisions
    2. Rare decisions
    3. Major decisions
    4. Minor decisions
    5. Policy decisions

133. Example of recurring decision is

    1. Determining sales quota
    2. Advertisement
    3. Raw material
    4. Finished product
    5. 1 and 2

134. All the decisions which involve great risk are called –

    1. Very risky decisions
    2. Risky decisions
    3. Recurring decisions
    4. Rare decisions
    5. Major decisions

135. Example of very risky decisions is

    1. Pricing policy of enterprise
    2. Change the price of product

3. Appointment of marketing executive
4. 1 and 3
5. **1, 2 and 3**

136. Which type of decisions is having minimum risk ?

    1. Very risky decision
    2. **Less risky decision**
    3. Important decision
    4. Rare decision
    5. Vital decision

137. Focus of selling activity is always on –

    1. **Seller's need**
    2. Producer's need
    3. Government need
    4. Taxable need
    5. Competitor's need

138. Focus of marketing activity is always on –

    1. **Consumer's need**
    2. Producer's need
    3. Government need
    4. Taxable need
    5. None of these

139. What is the step involved in marketing concept ?

    1. Customer need
    2. Integrated marketing
    3. Profit through customer satisfaction
    4. 1 and 3
    5. **1, 2 and 3**

140. Which was the period of sales oriented stage ?

1. 1901 – 1920
2. 1930 – 1950
3. 1900 – 1927
4. 2000 – 2008
5. 1957 – 1992

141. Products which are used in producing other goods and services are called –

    1. Industrial goods
    2. Consumer goods
    3. Household goods
    4. Shopping goods
    5. Speciality goods

142. What is one of the classifications of industrial products ?

    1. Production material
    2. Production supplies
    3. Production facilities
    4. Management materials
    5. All of above

143. What is the main classifications of industrial product ?

    1. Production material
    2. Production supplies
    3. Goods management material
    4. Production facilities and equipments
    5. All of above

144. Name the subheads of production material under industrial product –

    1. Raw material
    2. Semi finished goods
    3. Fabricating goods
    4. All of above

5. None of these

145. Example of raw material under production material is

   1. Sugarcane for sugar industry
   2. Cotton for textile industry
   3. Natural rubber for parts of T.V.
   4. All of above
   5. 1 & 3

146. Another name of semifinished products is

   1. Work
   2. Work in progress
   3. Progress of work
   4. Slow progress
   5. None of these

147. The goods which are manufactured by one industrial unit and used by another industrial unit without any processing are called

   1. Raw material
   2. Semi finished
   3. Production
   4. Production supplies
   5. Fabricating goods

148. Examples of fabricating goods are –

   1. Speaker for T.V.
   2. Tyre and tube
   3. Pen and ink
   4. 1 and 3
   5. 1, 2 and 3

149. The goods which are necessary for the operation of industrial unit are called –

1. Production material
2. Production supplies
3. Supplies
4. Material
5. Facilities

150. .... helps in process of production.

   1. Production facilities and equipments
   2. Material
   3. Supplies
   4. Raw material
   5. Semi finished

151. Example of production supplies is

   1. Coal
   2. Gas
   3. Nut-Bolt
   4. Cleaning material
   5. All of above

152. Example of production facilities I s

   1. Plant
   2. Building
   3. Furniture
   4. All of above
   5. None of these

153. What is the bases of difference between consumer goods and industrial goods ?

   1. Nature of customers
   2. Number of customers
   3. Nature of demand
   4. Product analysis
   5. All of above

154. Expansion of product mix states –

    1. Increase in the number of product lines
    2. Increase the number of product items in product line
    3. More companies
    4. Maximum exploftation of plant
    5. 1 and 2

155. What is true of under product line ?

    1. It is important that under product line are not necessary to be related with the existing lines
    2. Its necessary that new product line should be as same as previous one
    3. Two products should be launched at a time
    4. 1 and 2
    5. 1, 2 and 3

156. What is one of the objectives of Expansion of product mix ?

    1. To assure regular demand
    2. To start the production of by product
    3. To increase market recognition
    4. To earn profits
    5. 1, 2 and 3

157. Contraction of product mix means –

    1. Reducing the number of product lines
    2. Reducing the number of product items in product line
    3. Increase production capacity
    4. Decrease production capacity
    5. 1 and 2

158. "The composite of all products offered for sale for sale by a firm" is called :

1. **Product mix**
2. Product line
3. Product
4. Product item
5. Special product

159. Single product is called

    1. Product mix
    2. **Product item**
    3. Product line
    4. Special product
    5. Normal product

160. All the product items of the same group are called :

    1. **Product line**
    2. Product mix
    3. Product grade
    4. Special product
    5. Normal product

161. Global marketing involves developing marketing strategies as if the world is one market. Which one of the following marketing mix variables is MOST difficult to standardize for global marketing ?

    1. Brand name
    2. Package
    3. **Media allocation**
    4. Labels
    5. None of these

162. When graphic products decided to go international with its marketing effort, it adopted a totally global approach. Which one of the following factors did GP MOST likely experience difficulty with as the firm applied a global strategy for marketing ?

1. Branding
2. Product characteristics
3. Packaging
4. **Advertising**
5. None of these

163. When products are introduced into one nation from another, acceptance is far more likely

1. If prices are set very low
2. When bribes are paid to local officials to aid distribution
3. **If there are similarities between the two customs**
4. If packaging is adjusted to match local customs
5. None of these

164. Which of the following is often used to raise revenue for a country and to product domestic products ?

1. A quota
2. A warning label
3. An embargo
4. **An import tariff**
5. None of these

165. The .... is the difference in value between a nation's export and its imports.

1. **Balance of payments**
2. Export / import ratio
3. Gross domestic product
4. Net trade value
5. None of these

166. JCB would look to which of the following factors to determine how trade barriers would affect its ability to market its earth moving equipment in various countries ?

1. **Political and legal forces**
2. Interpersonal forces
3. Social forces
4. Technological forces
5. None of these

167. Which of the following statements about technological forces in international marketing is TRUE ?

1. Television advertising can be used universally throughout the world
2. **Much of the technology used in industrialized regions of the world may be ill-suited for developing countries**
3. Because all countries have up-to-date postal services, direct mail advertising is always a viable option
4. Technology is generally not a problem in international marketing
5. None of these

168. USA chemicals' president is very excited about the possibility of the firm's British subsidiary having access to the entire EU. He realize that it will be some time before this area truly becomes one market, primarily because of differences in

1. Available advertising media
2. **Culture**
3. Law
4. Technology
5. None of these

169. Countries in the pacific rim encompass ……….. of the world's population.

1. 40%
2. 50%
3. **60%**
4. 70%

5. None of these

170. The lowest level of commitment to international marketing, and also the most flexible approach, is

    1. A joint venture
    2. Direct ownership
    3. Exporting
    4. Licensing
    5. None of these

171. Export agents

    1. Bring buyers and sellers from different countries together and collect a commission for arranging sales
    2. Purchase products from different companies and sell them to foreign countries
    3. Are specialists at understanding the needs of customers in foreign countries
    4. Aarange for licensing agreements between domestic and foreign countries
    5. None of these

172. Cuisinart Corporation owns the Spalding name but does not produce a single golf club or tennis ball. This arrangement could indicate what type of organizational structure for international marketing ?

    1. Exporting
    2. Tranding
    3. Joint venture
    4. Licensing
    5. None of these

173. Nuhitzu believes it has technological expertise to produce communication systems that will be the leaders around the

globe. Boston Electronics is widely regarded as having excellent management system and superior marketing programme The two might form .... to work together on a worldwide basis.

1. A licensing agreement
2. An export trading company
3. A joint agreement
4. **A strategic alliance**
5. None of these

174. Once a company makes a long term commitment to a foreign market that has promising political and economic environment, what becomes a possibility ?

1. Exporting
2. Joint venture
3. Limited exporting
4. **Direct ownership**
5. None of these

175. ICI has subsidiaries in many countries. ICI is

1. An exporter
2. A licensing company
3. A trading company
4. **A multinational company**
5. None of these

176. Body Shop and Benetton are examples of companies which have employed .... as a market entry strategy.

1. **Franchising**
2. Exporting
3. Joint venture
4. Licensing
5. None of these

177. Which approach to international marketing involves least risk and minimum effort ?

1. Licensing
2. Exporting
3. Franchising
4. Joint venturing
5. None of these

178. The most suitable advertisement media for a Departmental store is

   1. National news paper
   2. Television
   3. Holdings
   4. Radio
   5. Internet

179. Direct mail advertising is suitable for

   1. Share brocker
   2. Hotel
   3. Doctor
   4. Manufacturer
   5. Serviceman

180. Sandwitch Board Advertisement is not suitable for

   1. Bread
   2. Cold drink
   3. Car
   4. Circus
   5. Play

181. When a number of advertise ments are published in a news paper in series at a regular   intervals, it is called

   1. Classified advertisement
   2. News type advertisement
   3. Teaser advertisement
   4. Outdoor advertisement
   5. None of above

182. 'Catalogue' is generally used in

   1. Personal advertising
   2. Direct mail advertising
   3. Classified advertising
   4. Window shopping
   5. None of these

183. Which of the following is a method od sales promotion ?

   1. Free gifts to consumers
   2. Discount coupons
   3. Price reduction
   4. Premium product
   5. All of above

184. The performance of actual selling activity is called

   1. Personal selling
   2. Sales promotion
   3. Sales campaign
   4. All of above
   5. None of these

185. Which is an activity of personal selling ?

   1. To sell the product to consumer directly
   2. To train the sales force
   3. To maintain the sales records
   4. To avoid consumer satisfaction
   5. 1, 2 & 3

186. Which is the irregular programme of a sales campaign ?

   1. Personal selling
   2. Advertisement

3. Sales promotion
4. Discounts
5. None of these

187. A salesman must be honest towards :

1. Product
2. Consumer only
3. Employer only
4. Sales promotion
5. Selling area

188. A particular growing of customers and prospects assigned to a salesman for his sales activities is known as :

1. Market
2. Product
3. Sales zone
4. Sales territories
5. Selling area

189. A specific sales target assigned to a particular salesman is described as –

1. Sales volume
2. Sales goal
3. Sales quota
4. Sales target
5. All of these

190. Can a manufacturer eliminates completely the rises involved in marketing ?

1. Yes
2. In special conditions
3. No
4. Can't say
5. May be or not

191. What is the main philosophy behind marketing concept now a days ?

    1. **Customer is king**
    2. Customer is fool
    3. Customer is brave
    4. Customer is loyal
    5. Customer is customer

192. Every company make efforts to provide the goods and services to the consumer at –

    1. **Right time**
    2. Right place
    3. As per their taste
    4. 1 and 3
    5. 1, 2 and 3

193. In general sense marketing research is ……….. regarding goods and services.

    1. **Collection**
    2. Summary
    3. Analysis of the data
    4. None of these
    5. 1, 2 and 3

194. Who said "Marketing research may be defined as the application of scientific method to the solution of marketing problems" ?

    1. **Luck, Wales and Taylor**
    2. Prof. Richard D. Crisp
    3. Parashar P.K.
    4. Tousley
    5. Clark & Clark

195. The main objects of marketing research is to

   1. Prepare market policies
   2. Amend market policies
   3. Prepare market strategies
   4. Amend market strategies
   5. All of above

196. Scope of marketing research is

   1. Very wide
   2. Low
   3. Narrow
   4. Simply wide
   5. None of these

197. Who said "Marketing research is a systematic attempt to get information useful in solving marketing problems"?

   1. Clark and Clark
   2. Pankaj Parashar
   3. Lorel, Wales & Taylor
   4. Prof. Richar D. Crisp
   5. Sh. Lalu Prasad Yadav

198. Prof. Richard D. Crisp has included .... in marketing research.

   1. Products
   2. Services research
   3. Market research
   4. Advertisement research
   5. All of above

199. What is the concept included in marketing research?

   1. Research of product and services
   2. Research on markets

3. Research on sales
4. Research on sales methods and policies
5. None of these

200. Name the concept which is meant to study the satisfaction of customers.

1. Research
2. Research of products and services
3. Research on markets
4. Research on sales methods and policies
5. **None of above**

201. Marketing includes the entire process of –

1. Satisfying the needs of consumer
2. Satisfying the wants of consumers
3. Satisfying taxes
4. Satisfying products
5. **1 and 2**

202. Who said "Marketing is the performance of those business activities that direct the flow of goods and services from producer to consumer." ?

1. **American marketing association**
2. Prof. Clark
3. Prof. Pankaj Parashar
4. Prof. Philip Kotler
5. Manmohan Singh

203. Marketing is the process of –

1. Planning
2. Organizing
3. Directing
4. Motivating and other activities
5. **All of above**

204. Who said "Management is the art of getting things done through and with people in formally   organized groups." ?

   1.   **Harold D. Kanntz**
   2.   Henry Fayol
   3.   James L. Lundy
   4.   Theo Haimann
   5.   Stanely Vance

205. New product idea generation can come from –

   1.   Distributor
   2.   Supplier
   3.   Customer
   4.   Competitors
   5.   **All of above**

206. The screening stage of the new product development process is used to –

   1.   **Eliminate undesirable ideas**
   2.   Generate new product ideas
   3.   Ideas
   4.   Determine potential profits from the new product
   5.   Determine how long the test market should run

207. Standard test markets have characteristic, that include –

   1.   Taking proper care
   2.   Taking along time to complete
   3.   Being very costly
   4.   Giving competitors a look at the new product
   5.   **2, 3 and 5**

208. What are the different stages of the product life cycle ?

1. Creation & Development
2. **Product Development, Introduction, Growth, Maturity, Decline**
3. Corruption growth maturity decline
4. Innovative growth decline
5. Introduction growth maturity

209. A company's internal new product development process is the only way for them to get new   products

1. True
2. True when new product it an FMCG
3. **False**
4. False when company has critical product line
5. True in some special cases

210. Because the new product development process is so through, new consumers packaged goods   rarely fail in today's market place :

1. True
2. True when development process is very slow
3. True when there is no packaged food
4. **False**
5. False in case of monopoly

211. Fads are –

1. Food products
2. A basic distinctive made of expression
3. **Fashions that enter quickly, are adopted with great appeal, peak early and decline very   slowly**
4. A currently accepted
5. Fashions that enter quickly, are adopted with great appeal, peak early and decline very fast

212. When a product reaches maturity, you should –

1. Offer product extension
2. Offer product extension, service, warranty
3. Offer a basic product
4. Phase out weak items
5. **Diversity brand and models**

213. Controlled test markets usually cost less and take less time than standard test markets :

   1. **True**
   2. True when all competitors are of same nature
   3. When all the producers produces the same product
   4. False
   5. False when market is of monopoly nature

214. Many companies, to save time over 'simuitaneous' product development, have adopted 'sequential product development' :

   1. True
   2. When product is industrial
   3. True if all consumers are educated
   4. **False**
   5. False if customer is fruit seller

215. The there major personal influences believed decision process are :

   1. Perception motives and attitudes
   2. Personality learning and perception
   3. Emographic situational and attitudes
   4. **Situational lifestyle and demographic**
   5. None of these

216. The purchase of …………….. is least likely to be affected by demographic factors.

   1. A car
   2. **Table salt**

3. A computer for home use
4. Fast food
5. None of these

217. Buyers tend to remember information inputs that support their beliefs and forget inputs that support their beliefs and forget inputs that to do. This is known as selective

1. Exposure
2. Distortion
3. **Retention**
4. Information
5. None of these

218. If a consumer receives information that is inconsistent with her or his feelings or belief, the consumer may alter this information. This is known as selective :

1. Exposure
2. **Distortion**
3. Retention
4. Information
5. None of these

219. Psychological forces that influence where a person purchases products on a regular basis are called :

1. Convenience responses
2. **Patronage motives**
3. Shopping motives
4. Pattern responses
5. None of these

220. A depth interview is MOST likely to be used to :

1. Alter a buyer's attitudes toward a product
2. Influence a buyer's perceptions of a product
3. **Discover a buyer's motives**

4. Increase a buyer's knowledge of a product
5. None of these

221. Having used both Rexona and Denim deodorants, Anna feels that sure is a good product and the one that best meets her needs. She has formed ………….. about sure.

1. A motive
2. An evoked set
3. A cognition
4. **An attitude**
5. None of above

222. A consumer's buying decisions are affected in part by the people around him or her. These   people and the forces they exert on a buyer are called

1. Motivational influences
2. **Social factors**
3. Roles
4. Personality influences
5. None of these

223. Damien is torn between buying a new swing set for his children and buying a new set of   Wilson golf clubs for himself. He is experiencing :

1. Attitude formation
2. Belief assessment
3. **Role inconsistency**
4. Cognitive dissonance
5. None of these

224. Which one of the following is MOST likely to be a product for which both the purchasing   decision and the brand decision are strongly influenced by reference groups ?

1. Canned peaches

2. Instant coffee
3. Jeans
4. Bed linen
5. None of these

225. The car company developed a concept statement "An inexpensive subcompact 'green' car appealing to environmentally conscious people who want practical transportation and low pollution." This concept statement would be used

1. To develop concepts
2. For concept testing
3. To prepare for idea screening
4. To help generate new ideas
5. None of these

226. How does a company estimate sales ?

1. It examines past sales history of similar products
2. It conducts market research to survey consumers
3. It discusses manufacturing capacity with the plant manager
4. a and b
5. None of these

227. The strategy used during maturity to attempt to increase the consumption of the current product is called

1. Customer modification
2. Market modification
3. Product modification
4. Marketing mix modification
5. None of these

228. As a product manager on a product life cycle, what should you specifically do to best market your product ?

1. Defend against competitive marketing lastics

2. Prepare to discontinue the product
3. **Modify the product market and the marketing mix**
4. Increase sampling programs
5. None of these

229. Setting prices as low as possible typically supports which of the following marketing objectives ?

1. Survival
2. Current profit maximization
3. **Market share leadership**
4. Product quality leadership
5. None of these

230. Finance requirement to carry on marketing activities is known as :

1. Finance
2. **Marketing finance**
3. Social finance
4. Long term finance
5. Short term finance

231. Which is the starting point of marketing process ?

1. Discovery of needs
2. Wants of consumer
3. Making fraud of consumers
4. All of above
5. **1 and 2**

232. What is the ending point of marketing process ?

1. Discovery of needs
2. **Satisfaction of needs and wants of consumers**
3. Wants of consumers
4. Making fool of consumers
5. All of above

233. The method which is used by the firm for purchasing new assets, when they don't have adequate funds is called

    1. Cash purchases
    2. Purchase
    3. Lease out
    4. Installment payment method
    5. All of above

234. Who said "Advertising is a paid form of non-personal presentation of the idea, goods or services by an identified sponsor" ?

    1. Richard Buskirk
    2. Prof. Aditya Sharma
    3. Prof. Weed
    4. Philip Kotler

235. What is one of the function of advertisement ?

    1. Primary function
    2. Secondary function
    3. Economic function
    4. All of above

236. "To introduce new goods and services to the world of consumers" is the main object of –

    1. Government
    2. Enemy country
    3. Advertising
    4. Products

237. Advantages of advertisement has been broadly classified as :

    1. Advantages to middleman
    2. Advantages to consumers
    3. Advantages to society

4. **All of above**

238. What is one of the advantages of advertisement to producers ?

    1. Stability
    2. Increase in sales
    3. Increase in profits
    4. Increase in goodwill
    5. **All of above**

239. Increase in sale results :

    1. Increase in profit
    2. Increase in competition
    3. Increase in fraud
    4. Increase in dignity
    5. **All of above**

240. What is one of the advantages of advertisement to consumers ?

    1. Knowledge of new product
    2. Convenience purchasing
    3. Saving of time
    4. Increase in cheating
    5. **1, 2 and 3**

241. Advertising research helps in –

    1. **Selecting suitable media for advertisement**
    2. Selecting salesman
    3. Selecting transport
    4. Selecting channels
    5. None of these

242. Marketing research is a gift of

    1. Modern concept of marketing

2. Classing concept of marketing
3. Traditional concept of marketing
4. Old concept of marketing
5. **Basis concept of marketing**

243. Example of less risky decisions is

1. Appointment of sales representative
2. Change of colour
3. Change of packing
4. Change of weight
5. **All of above**

244. Which decision decides the marketing policy of enterprise ?

1. **Policy decision**
2. Rare decision
3. Rerest decision
4. Minor decision
5. Major decision

245. Example of policy decision is

1. Selection of channel of distribution
2. Selection of media of advertisement
3. Selection of methods of sales promotion
4. **All of above**
5. None of above

246. Which of the following is a types of techniques of decision making ?

1. Tranditional method
2. Rare method
3. Rearest method
4. Scientific method
5. **1 and 4**

247. Under which technique of decision making method of decision making is based on symptomatic diagnosis ?

    1. **Traditional method**
    2. Rare method
    3. Medical method
    4. Scientific method
    5. Analyse method

248. Which of the following is one of the aspects of the process of scientific method ?

    1. Ascertaining the problem
    2. Analyse the problem
    3. Development of alternative solution
    4. Selection of best alternative solutions
    5. **All of the above**

249. What is the importance of marketing in India Economy ?

    1. Increase in employment opportunities
    2. Balanced growth of the country
    3. Increase in per capital income
    4. Increase in the sale of goods
    5. **All of above**

250. What are the main functions of marketing ?

    1. Marketing research
    2. Product planning and development
    3. Buying and assembling of goods
    4. Packing, packaging & labeling
    5. **All of above**

251. Products are the foundation store of any marketing programme therefore .... is very important.

    1. Product planning
    2. Product

3. Product development
4. Creation
5. **1 and 3**

252. What are the decisions included in product planning and development ?

1. What to produce
2. How to pack the product
3. Prize fixing
4. Size
5. **All of above**

253. The marketing department determines the requirements of customers and pass on this information to following departments :

1. Production department
2. H.R. department
3. Purchase department
4. Security department
5. **1 and 3**

254. The term "assembling" can be described in different senses. How many are they ?

1. One
2. **Two**
3. Fifteen
4. Twenty
5. Hundred

255. Selling is very complicated function because of the

1. Market situation
2. Substitute available in the market
3. Serve competition in the market
4. 1 and 2
5. **1, 2 and 3**

256. Liquid material like wine and squash should be packed in –

   1. Cloth
   2. Paper
   3. Bottles
   4. Mud pots
   5. 2, 3 and 4

257. Packaging includes –

   1. Container
   2. Wrapper
   3. Bottles
   4. Cartoons
   5. All of above

258. A trade mark is a legal term which refers to a brand registered under :

   1. Trade and merchandise marks act 1958
   2. Indian companies act 1956
   3. Indian partnership act 1932
   4. IPC
   5. All of above

259. Which is one of the example of brand ?

   1. Rath vanaspati
   2. Colgate toothpaste
   3. Four square cigarettes
   4. Tata tea
   5. All of above

260. Physical means of carrying goods is –

   1. Transportation

2. Communication
3. Warehouse
4. Copyright
5. None of these

261. What is the risk involved in business ?

1. Natural risk
2. Competitive risk
3. Human risk
4. Political risk
5. All of above

262. It is very difficult to eliminate the risk but it can be –

1. Increased
2. Minimised
3. Scheduled
4. Property managed
5. None of these

263. No business and industrial enterprise can achieve its marketing objectives in the absence of –

1. Marketing research
2. Product research
3. Consumer research
4. Simple research
5. Advance research

264. Which concept signifies the importance of making research ?

1. Production of products
2. New use of products
3. Knowledge of demand
4. Planned production
5. All of above

265. Marketing research explores the possibility of selling a .... product into a market.

    1. New
    2. Old
    3. Traditional
    4. Searched
    5. FMGG

266. How production of new product helps enterprises ?

    1. Capturing the market
    2. Loose the market
    3. Research the market
    4. Create the market
    5. Leave the market

267. Wide publicity of new uses of product can –

    1. Create new market
    2. Create new customer
    3. Save tax
    4. Make fraud dealings
    5. 1 and 2

268. Which of the following studies analysis the nature of customers ?

    1. Important information about customers
    2. Important information about market
    3. Important information about product
    4. Important information about competitors
    5. Important information about government

269. Producers use to send their product to customers with the help of –

1. **Doordarshan T.V. channel**
2. Distribution channel
3. Midway channel
4. Market channel
5. Competitors channel

270. Under which important researches the product and services offered by competitors ?

    1. **Existence in competitive situation**
    2. Existence in market
    3. Existence in product line
    4. Existence in product planning
    5. None of above

271. ……….. can adjust demand and supply of products of company.

    1. Planning production
    2. Nonplanned production
    3. Total production
    4. **Average production**
    5. Marginal production

272. The consumer may discard the product tomorrow –

    1. Which they prefer today
    2. **Which they hate today**
    3. Which is in demand
    4. Which is available in market
    5. None of above

273. What is the basic fundamental of marketing management ?

    1. The objectives of the enterprise must be the maximum satisfaction of consumer needs
    2. Maximum retail fraud with customer

3. Efforts must be made to maximize the profits through maximum sales
4. All of above
5. **1 and 3**

274. How many fundamentals of marketing management has been initiated by William J. Stanton ?

   1. Seven
   2. Ten
   3. **Two**
   4. Three
   5. Four

275. Marketing management is the combination of –

   1. Analysis
   2. Planning
   3. Implementation
   4. Control
   5. **All of above**

276. Rule of P's consist of …….. P's.

   1. **Product**
   2. Price
   3. Promotion
   4. Place
   5. Property

277. 4 P's does not stand for –

   1. Product
   2. Price
   3. Promotion
   4. Place
   5. **Property**

278. The most common and ultimate object of all business activities is –

    1. **To earn maximum profit**
    2. Cost minimization
    3. Independence
    4. Rapid industrialization
    5. None of these

279. In which period marketing management was not considered to be very important in India ?

    1. **Before independence**
    2. After independence
    3. On independence
    4. In 2000
    5. In 2000 – 2001

280. What is the percentage of population of India living in Rural areas ?

    1. 20 per cent
    2. **72.2 per cent**
    3. 68 per cent
    4. 40 per cent
    5. 70 per cent

281. Green Revolution shows growth in –

    1. Modern fertilizers
    2. Irrigation facilities
    3. Improvement in agricultural technique
    4. Use of improved seeds
    5. **All of above**

282. India is lacking in the development of techniques of marketing because –

    1. Lack of marketing personel

2. Lack of marketing research facilities
3. Attitude of Indian industrialists
4. Attitude of Indian consumers
5. **All of above**

283. India have a shortage of marketing personels because of –

   1. Less number of institutes
   2. Lack in learning capacity
   3. Lack of proper planning
   4. **1 and 3**
   5. 1, 2 and 3

284. In India we don't have fundamental research facility that's why we are lacking in –

   1. **Market research**
   2. Market
   3. Marketing
   4. Competition
   5. All of above

285. A producer who wants to carry his own marketing research, he face the problem of –

   1. Qualified people
   2. Trained researchers
   3. Infrastructure
   4. Government obligations
   5. **1 and 2**

286. Most of the industrialists in India do not make their efforts for the development of market because –

   1. Government Regulations
   2. Their attitude does not allow it
   3. The cost of product will increase
   4. It will reduce profit margin

5. **3 and 4**

287. Indian industrialists through that research on following topic / field is useless :

    1. Taste of consumer
    2. Needs of consumer
    3. Wants of consumer
    4. Behavior of consumer
    5. **All of above**

288. How the attitude of India consumers affect the marketing research ?

    1. The generally do not co-operate
    2. They do not reply the questions asked in marketing research programme
    3. **They are criminals**
    4. They are careless
    5. 1 and 2

289. Techniques of marketing management has not been developed because of

    1. **The lacking of effective product planning**
    2. Defective product
    3. More industries
    4. Government regulation
    5. All of above

290. Problem of defective channels of distribution arise because of —

    1. Unorganized distribution sector
    2. Improper planning
    3. No needs
    4. No transport
    5. **1 and 2**

291. What are the causes of high marketing cost ?

   1. Advertisement charges
   2. Packing expence
   3. Trade mark chargers
   4. Transportation cost
   5. **All of above**

292. Marketing management has to perform .... Functions in marketing products.

   1. Solo
   2. Two
   3. **Many**
   4. Twelve
   5. None of these

293. What is the main function performed by marketing management ?

   1. Planning
   2. Organizing
   3. Directing
   4. Motivating
   5. **All of above**

294. Which of the following is one of the types of marketing objectives ?

   1. Short term
   2. Permanent
   3. Artificial
   4. Long term
   5. **1 and 4**

295. Marketing plan must be quite clear so that :

1. Activities can be directed
2. Plan must be kept clear and updated
3. Goods can be sold
4. Shops can be opened
5. All of above

296. Which of the following is a description of a product in the growth phase of its product life cycle ?

1. Peak season - high profit
2. Peak season high profits, low cost per customer
3. Declining sales, declining profits, high cost per customer
4. Low sales, negative profits high cost per customer
5. **Rapidly rising sales, rising profits, average cost per customer**

297. "Fashion" is the currently accepted or popular style in a given field :

1. False in case of clothes related to old people
2. False if old fashion clothes
3. **True**
4. False
5. True in case of teenagers

298. To understand product planning properly it is necessary to understand the individual meaning of :

1. Product
2. By product
3. Planning
4. Maximum
5. **1 & 3**

299. "Deciding what is to be done in future" is called –

1. **Planning**

2. Plan
3. Plane
4. Plain
5. Please

300. "Deciding a particular product which will be produced by the enterprise" is called

    1. Planning
    2. Producer's planning
    3. Product planning
    4. Planman
    5. Preference plan

301. Match the items of List - I with items of List - II and select the correct code of matching :

List - I
(a) Market Leader
(b) Market Challenger
(c) Market Follower
(d) Market Nicher

List - II
(i) Avoid hostile attacks on rivals
(ii) Attack the market leader
(iii) Provide high level of specialisation
(iv) Attack the market

Code :

	(a)	(b)	(c)	(d)
(A)	4	2	1	3
(B)	2	2	3	1
(C)	3	1	4	2
(D)	1	3	4	2

302. Which of the statements are correct ? Select correct code.

Statement (I) : Opinions can be described as the slow responses we might give to opinion poll questions about any issue.

Statement (II) : Attitudes are held with a greater degree of conviction, over longer duration and more likely to influence behaviour.

Statement (III) : Values are held more strongly than attitudes and underpin our attitudinal behaviour.

Code :

a. (I) and (II) **b. (II) and (III)** c. (I) and (III) d. (I), (II) and (III)

303. Which of the following is not a major aspect of digital marketing ?

a. Jurisdiction b. Ownership c. Security **d. Entertainment**

304. Which of the following statements are correct ? Select the correct code.

Statement (I) : Horizontal conflict between channel members is caused due to channel members impinge on the market territory of other intermediaries at different level.

Statement (II) : Vertical conflict is caused due to intense price competition, disagreement about promotional activities, attempts to bypass intermediary and distribute direct, differing expectations as to channel or intermediary performance.

Statement (III) : Hybrid channel conflict arises due to grey marketing.

Code :

1. (I) and (III)
2. (I) and (II)
3. **(II) and (III)**
4. (I), (II) and (III)

305. Which of the following statements are incorrect ? Indicate the correct code.

Statement (I) : As consumer's income increases, the percentage of income spent for food items decreases, for rent, fuel and light remains the same, for clothing remains the same and for sundries increases.

Statement (II) : Societal marketing period was from 1960 onwards.

Statement (III) : Our debt to social anthropology decreases more and more as we use qualitative market research approaches.

Statement (IV) : The economic concepts of perfect competition and matching of supply and demand underlie the marketing concept, particularly in relation to the concepts of the price at which goods are sold and quantity distributed.

Code :

a. (I) and (II)
b. **(II) and (III)**
c. (II) and (IV)
d. (I) and (IV)

306. When Walt Disney World's Magic kingdom lets customers visit a fairy kingdom, a pirate ship, or a haunted house, then what is marketed in this example ?
    a. Services   b. Events **c. Experiences**
    d. Ideas

307. Which one of the following statements is true according to VALS (Values and Life Styles) framework of psychographic segmentation ?
    a. The consumers who are primarily motivated by ideals are guided by knowledge and principles.
    b. consumers who are motivated by achievement look for knowledge and principles.
    c. The consumers who are motivated by self expression don't desire social or physical activity, variety, and risk.

d. The consumers who are motivated by achievement desire social or physical activity, variety, and risk.

308. From the following two statements of Assertion (A) and Reason (R), indicate the correct code :
   Assertion (A) : A transformational appeal of communication elaborates on a non-product related benefit or image.
   Reasoning (R) : Transformational appeals often do not attempt to stir up emotions that will motivate purchase.
   Code :

1. (A) and (R) both are correct.
2. **(A) is correct (R) is not correct.**
3. (A) is not correct (R) is correct.
4. (A) and (R) both are incorrect.

309. Select the correct sequence for Hierarchy-of-effects model related to marketing communication :
   a. Awareness→Knowledge →Liking →Preference→Conviction →Purchase
   b. Knowledge →Awareness →Liking →Conviction →Preference →Purchase
   c. Awareness →Liking →Knowledge →Conviction →Preference →Purchase
   d. Liking →Awareness →Knowledge →Preference →Conviction →Purchase

310. Match the items of List - I with the items of List - II and denote the code of correct matching :

List - I
(A) Basic Product
(B) Expected Product
(C) Augmented Product
(D) Potential Product

List - II
(i) Set of attributes and conditions buyers normally expect

(ii) Possible augmentation and transformation the product might undergo in future
(iii) Exceed customer expectations
(iv) Converting core benefits into product

Code :

	(A)	(B)	(C)	(D)
a.	(iii)	(iv)	(i)	(ii)
b.	(i)	(iii)	(iv)	(ii)
c.	(i)	(iv)	(iii)	(ii)
d.	**(iv)**	**(i)**	**(iii)**	**(ii)**

311. Who said "The planning direction and control of all stages in the life cycle of a product from the time of its removal from the company's line of product is known as product planning" ?

    1. **Mason and rath**
    2. Johnson
    3. William J. Stanton
    4. Prof. Pankaj Parashar
    5. Prof. Akshita Sharma

312. Product planning is to take decisions regarding –

    1. Which product must be produced ?
    2. Which new product must be developed ?
    3. What expansion or contraction must be made ?
    4. How black marketing can be initiated
    5. **1, 2 and 3**

313. What is one of the main elements of product planning ?

    1. Research before production
    2. Possibility of the production of product
    3. Decision for the change in the product line

4. Elimination of unprofitable product
5. **All of above**

314. Research before production helps in deciding about –

1. Quality of product
2. Size of product
3. Design of product
4. Colour of product
5. **All of above**

315. Decision for the change in the product line includes –

1. Decision regarding existing product
2. Decision for corruption
3. Decision regarding new product
4. Decision for the theft of tax
5. **1 and 3**

316. What is one of the bases of the importance of product planning ?

1. Starting point of marketing programme
2. Symbol of managerial ability
3. To meet social responsibilities
4. Helpful in facing competition
5. **All of above**

317. Who said "Product planning is the starting point for the entire marketing programme" ?

1. **William J. Stanton**
2. Dr. B. D. Sharma
3. Prof. Pankaj Parashar
4. Prof. Philip Kotler
5. Marshal

318. Product planning is not an activity, it is a –

1. Boom
2. Development
3. **Process**
4. Creation
5. Planning

319. Who said "Product development encompasses the technical activities of product research, engineering and design"?

    1. **Willian J. Stanton**
    2. Limpson and Darling
    3. Prof. Bhagwan Dass Sharma
    4. Lal Krishna Adwani
    5. Prof. Pankaj Parashar

320. What is one of the main elements of product development?

    1. To discover the feasibility of the production of product
    2. To develop the quality of product
    3. To develop different models
    4. To select the best model
    5. **All of above**

321. What is one of the principles of product development?

    1. Principle of standardization
    2. Principle of simplification
    3. Principle of specialization
    4. Principle of double entry
    5. **1, 2 and 3**

322. Which principle stresses upon the fact that these must be predetermined standards for the product?

    1. Principle of Accountancy
    2. Principle of Marketing
    3. **Principle of standardisation**
    4. Principle of MBA College

5. None of above

323. Which principle stresses that production process must be as simple as possible ?

  1. **Principle of simplification**
  2. Principle of justification
  3. Principle of marketing
  4. 1 and 3
  5. 1, 2 and 3

324. What is one of the main advantages of product development ?

  1. Best quality products
  2. Market expansion
  3. Maximum satisfaction to customer
  4. Increase in profits
  5. **All of above**

325. The assistant category manager was told to use cost plus pricing to evaluate the profit potential of new products. This involves

  1. Setting prices to reach a specific rate of return
  2. **Adding standard markup to the cost of the product**
  3. Pricing products with the buyer's sense of value in mind
  4. Basing the prices on what the competition charges
  5. None of these

326. Before setting his prices, Zach conducted a market research study to learn what consumers would pay. Zach appears to be using which type of pricing method ?

  1. Cost plus
  2. Target profit
  3. **Value based**
  4. Going rate

5. None of these

327. When automobile manufacturers offer options in specially priced deals, they are practicing a   form of

1. Product line pricing
2. **Product bundle pricing**
3. Captive product pricing
4. By product pricing
5. None of these

328. Which, if any, of the following are reasons producers use intermediaries ?

1. Because of their greater efficiency in making goods available to target markets
2. Because of their contacts and experience with retailers
3. Because of their specialization in delivery goods as needed
4. **All 1, 2 and 3**
5. None of these

329. Which one of the following statements BEST characterizes marketing research ?

1. Research is a continuous process, providing a constant flow of information
2. **Research is conducted on a special project basis**
3. Research is performed when routine information is required
4. Research is the basis for making recurring marketing decisions
5. None of these

330. In the previous three years, four studies have been conducted on the characteristics of Tyrone Brick's clients. As the firm seeks to put together a report showing trends in this area, it has a hard time

locating the information contained in these study reports. This firm seems to need :

1. A marketing research manager
2. **A marketing databank**
3. Survey research
4. Primary data
5. None of these

331. An intuitive manager could best be described as one who :

1. Uses scientific problem solving
2. Eliminates uncertainty in decision making
3. Searches out facts and data systematically
4. **Uses personal knowledge and experience to make decision**
5. None of these

332. If Master Foods Ltd known that its market share in Ireland has dropped 13 percent in the first quarter of the year but does not know what night have contributed to this decline, it is in which stage of the marketing research process ?

1. Hypothesis development
2. Symptom identification
3. **Problem identification**
4. Data interpretation
5. None of these

333. Suppose marketers at Lever Brothers are trying to determine whether the use of money off coupons for detergent was the reason for a sales increase in a particular store. The type of study conducted to answer this question would best be :

1. Exploratory
2. Descriptive
3. **Casual**
4. Qualitiative

5. None of these

334. Marks and Spencer wants to learn about consumer attitudes toward mail order purchases and   conducts a study to acquire this information, this study would best be classified as collecting .... Data.

1. Casual
2. Experimental
3. **Primary**
4. Secondary
5. None of these

335. When working on a job placement for a local retailer. Joan Halverson was sent to the library   to look up data on population forecasts for Scotland. The population information she found would be considered .... data.

1. Primary
2. **Secondary**
3. Syndicated research
4. Exploratory
5. None of these

336. Primary data are BEST described as the :

1. First batch of data collected for a specific study
2. **Data that are observed, recorded or collected from respondents**
3. Data that were compiled for some purpose other than the study current study
4. Data that are collected from a computerized data base
5. None of these

337. Which of the following is a mode of advertisements ?

1. Press advertisement
2. Outdoor advertisement

3. Entertainment advertisement
4. Mail advertisement
5. **All of above**

338. Which is not a part of branch concept ?

    1. **Product Mix**
    2. Brand image
    3. Brand Franchise
    4. Brand Recognition

339. An evolution of the Marketing discipline includes

    1. Brand Management
    2. Selling
    3. Mass Production
    4. **All of the above**

340. Re-defining business relationship includes

    1. Formation of business network
    2. Re-intermediation
    3. Dis-intermediation
    4. **All of the above**

341. What is the use of the Internet in Marketing ?

    1. In Product and Market Extension
    2. In Market Testing
    3. In Market Research
    4. **All of the above**

342. On-line Marketing includes

    1. Reason-orientation of on-line advertising
    2. Non Intrusivenses of on-line advertising
    3. Spatialty of on-line marketing
    4. **All of the above**

343. What is the advantages of on-line marketing ?

1. Making the location of Marketing Irrelevant
2. Increasing feedback
3. Making the size of Marketer Irrelevant
4. **All of the above**

344. Which is the barriers to on-line Marketing ?

1. Security
2. Infrastructural Barries
3. Customers Resistance
4. **All of the above**

345. Which of the following factors affects to the planning of marketing programme ?

1. Marketing Strategy
2. Marketing Mix
3. Demand Variable
4. **All of the above**

346. Which factors determines the building up of a sales organization ?

1. Size of the Unit
2. Organisation Policy of the Management
3. Traditions and customs
4. **All of the above**

347. Which is / are the element of Promotional Mix ?

1. Public Relation
2. Trade Faires and Exhibitions
3. Advertising
4. **All of the above**

348. .... marketing is a new way of performing the task of marketing, made feasible by the advent of new technology, namely the Internet

    1. Rural Marketing
    2. On-line Marketing
    3. Green Marketing
    4. Social Marketing

349. Which is the barriers to the adoption of online Marketing ?

    1. Lack of availability of skills
    2. Lack of availability of funds
    3. Lack of availability of technology
    4. Art of recording

350. Using the Power of online networks, computer communications and digital interactive media to achieve marketing and business objectives, is called

    1. Tel-net and internet
    2. Internet
    3. Securities
    4. None of these

351. Which is not a part of Promotional Media ?

    1. Cost
    2. Publication
    3. Printing
    4. Broadcasting out-of-home

352. The principle function of an electronic market is to facilitate the search for the

    1. Required Product or Service

2. Required Marketing
3. Required Market
4. All of the above

353. The marketing concept involves

1. Organisation Integration
2. Competition Orientation
3. Customer Orientation
4. **All of the above**

354. Modern Marketing consists

1. Merketing Strategy and research
2. Marketing effectiveness
3. Brand Management
4. **All of the above**

355. A brand is a

1. Product Plan
2. Product Cost
3. Quality
4. **Product or Service Name**

356. A brand includes

1. Combination of Name and Symbol
2. Design
3. Symbol or Number or Words
4. **All of the above**

357. A brand is a name, term, symbol, design combination of these which identifies the goods or   services of one seller or group those sellers and differentiates them from of

1. Other marketing

2. **Other sellers**
3. Other market
4. Other product or services

358. What is one of the types of press advertisement ?

1. News paper
2. Magazines
3. Journals
4. Directories
5. **All of above**

359. Which of the following is a mode of outdoor advertisement ?

1. Posters
2. Sign boards
3. Sandwich advertisement
4. Transport advertisement
5. **All of the above**

360. Advertisements which comes under the category of Entertainment advertisement is

1. Cinema
2. Radio
3. Exhibitions
4. T.V.
5. **All of above**

361. A type of mail advertisement is

1. Radio
2. Sale bill
3. Magazines
4. Catalogue
5. **3 and 4**

362. Which is the element of modern marketing ?

    1. It emphasizes mutuality of benefit
    2. It is customer oriented
    3. It is operational
    4. All of the above

363. Which is the key feature / features of market as per Baket ?

    1. Full use of all the company's resources
    2. A long run perspective
    3. Start with the customer
    4. All of the above

364. "Marketing is a human activity directed at satisfying needs and wants through exchange process". Who said ?

    1. Philip Kotler
    2. Hansi L. V.
    3. Peter F. Drucker
    4. D. S. Pauler

365. The internet offers marketers a fast, versatile and inexpensive

    1. Communication medium
    2. Cost of production
    3. Cost of construction
    4. All of the above

366. Product line covers

    1. Departmental Stores
    2. One Price Retailer
    3. General retailer
    4. All of the above

367 Modern concept of marketing consists

1. Co-ordination
2. Decision
3. Responsibility towards customers
4. **All of the above**

368. Marketing refers to the

    1. Goods Distribution
    2. Goods and services are exchange to each other
    3. Sales of Product
    4. **All of the above**

369. Functions of marketing management consists

    1. Determination the marketing objects
    2. Marketing planning
    3. Marketing organization
    4. **All of the above**

370. Which is the task of advancing ?

    1. Providing information about the product
    2. Image building
    3. Behaviour rein forcement
    4. **All of the above**

371. Which is the selling tasks ?

    1. Outside order taking
    2. Inside order taking
    3. Product delivery
    4. **All of the above**

372. Which is the task of salesman ?

    1. Develop product and market knowledge
    2. Sales Pitch

3. Prospect for potential clients
4. **All of the above**

373. The procedure for segmenting the industrial markets is different than the

1. **Industrial Markets**
2. Business Markets
3. Consumer Markets
4. All of the above

374. To manage a business well is to manage its future, and to manage the future is to manage information, this statement is related to

1. **Effective Marketing Information**
2. Promotion
3. Price
4. Effective Sales Planning

375. Market Research on Pricing includes

1. Demand Elasticities
2. Perceived Prices
3. Cost Analysis
4. **All of the above**

376. Which concept of marketing is product oriented ?

1. **Old concept of marketing**
2. Entity concept of business
3. Modern concept of marketing
4. All of the above

377. Which concept of marketing is customer oriental ?

1. **Modern concept of marketing**

2. Entity concept
3. Old concept of marketing
4. All of the above

378. Which of the following is Marketing oriental ?

    1. Decentralised
    2. Consumer Consideration dominate
    3. Broad Product line
    4. **All of the above**

379. Marketing orientation consists

    1. Emphasis on market price rather than cost
    2. Market Research
    3. External influence dominate objectives
    4. **All of the above**

380. Which is the factor of Pricing decisions ?

    1. Controller
    2. Style and appearance prime consideration
    3. Flexibility in production
    4. **All of the above**

381. Which is the factor of pricing decisions ?

    1. Economic and Political Environment of the Country
    2. Trade Traditions
    3. Competition
    4. **All of the above**

382. Pricing objectives consists

    1. Price stabilization
    2. Targeted rate of return
    3. Skim the cream

4. **All of the above**

383. Which of the following is pricing objectives ?

    1. Market Penetration
    2. Market Share
    3. Competition
    4. **All of the above**

384. Pricing objectives is combination of

    1. Product Line Promotion
    2. Cash Recovery
    3. Profit Maximisation
    4. **All of the above**

385. Which of the following cost may be used for pricing decision ?

    1. Fixed Cost
    2. Average Cost
    3. Variable Cost
    4. **All of these**

386. Which one of the following is not element of marketing mix ?

    1. Fixed Cost
    2. Product
    3. Place
    4. **Plan**

387. The choice of marketing mix depends upon

    1. Marketing organization structure and information system
    2. Marketing objectives
    3. The marketing environment of the organization
    4. **All of the above**

388. The promotion mix involves to

   1. Advertising
   2. Sales Promotion
   3. Personal Selling
   4. **All of the above**

389. The factors that guide a marketer's decision in selecting a promotion mix which are

   1. Buyer readiness stage
   2. Overall marketing strategy
   3. Nature or the Product Market
   4. **All of the above**

390. Which one of the step is not included under the step of marketing programming process ?

   1. Developing the marketing mix
   2. Selection of market targets
   3. Setting objectives
   4. **Market response**

391. Marketing mix involves

   1. Product mix
   2. Promotion / Promotional mix
   3. Service mix
   4. **All of the above**

392. Marketing Planning consists

   1. Determination of Policies
   2. Marketing Programmes
   3. Setting Objectives
   4. **All of the above**

393. Sub-dividation marketing is called as

   1.   Market segmentation
   2.   Allocation of marketing
   3.   Decision of marketing
   4.   Only segmentation

394. Which is the element of marketing mix ?

   1.   Product
   2.   Promotion
   3.   Price
   4.   All of the above

395. Who developed the 4 P's of marketing ?

   1.   J.R. Betty
   2.   Hanson
   3.   McCarthy
   4.   Peter F. Drucker

396. Which is the first I's of Marketing mix per 'Mc Cathy' ?

   1.   Product
   2.   Promotion
   3.   Price
   4.   Place

397. Which is not the 'P' of marketing ?

   1.   Product
   2.   Promotion
   3.   Price
   4.   Policy

398. Which is the part of 'Product' Planning Image ?

1. Total Quality Management
2. Risk
3. Credibility
4. All of the above

399. Which of the following factor that after Pricing decisions ?

1. Cost of the Product
2. Product characteristics
3. Demand of the Product
4. Distribution Channels of the Product

400. Channels of distribution is known as

1. Trade Channel
2. Proper Channel
3. Path Channel
4. None of these

401. The concept of marketing mix involves to deliberate and careful choice of organization product, price, promotion and place strategies and

1. Policies
2. Planning
3. Concept
4. All of the above

402. Marketing characteristics are

1. Product market segmentation
2. Need based marketing strategy
3. Profit – orientation
4. All of the above

403. Marketing Environment System covers

1. Marketing Information System
2. Monitoring and Control System
3. Marketing Planning System
4. **All of the above**

404. Which is not a form of Internet Marketing ?

1. Online marketing
2. Internet advertising
3. e-Marketing
4. **Product Mix and Branding**

405. Marketing management is the process of product planning, pricing, promotion and .... along with the services to generate transaction that satisfies the organizational and user objectives.

1. **Distribution or Place**
2. Reward
3. Goals
4. None of these

406. Marketing planning concicts

1. Product Positioning
2. Market Segmentation
3. Distribution Network
4. **All of the above**

407. Elements of marketing planning is

1. It involves an analysis of past events and projection of future events
2. In envisages determination of the future course of marketing action
3. Marketing planning is a managerial function
4. **All of the above**

408. Which is a base of green marketing ?

   1. **Greenhouse gas reduction market**
   2. Capital Flow
   3. Programme
   4. All of the above

409. Market control process consists

   1. Formation of Performance standard
   2. Performance Appraisal
   3. Correcting Deviations
   4. **All of the above**

410. Brand concept not includes

   1. **Digital marketing**
   2. Brand name
   3. Brand identity and value
   4. Brand personality

411. The marketing concerns requires both fixed capital and

   1. **Working Capital**
   2. Long-term-Capital
   3. Share Capital
   4. Flexible Capital

412. The marketing concerns generally taps three sources for financing its activities there are

   1. Owned Capital
   2. Trade Credit
   3. Bank Credit
   4. **All of the above**

413. Which is the problem of marketing communication ?

1. Distance
2. Hidden sources and data
3. Lack of trust
4. **All of the above**

414. In marketing 'SEM' means

    1. **Search-Engine-Marketing**
    2. Strategy-Engine-Money
    3. Sales-Engine-Management
    4. Sales-even-Money

415. Which of the following is not factors of the demand variable, according to Philip Kotler ?

    1. **Environment Variable**
    2. Competition Variable
    3. Customer Variable
    4. All of the above

416. Modern Marketing includes

    1. Digital Marketing
    2. Social Marketing
    3. Green Marketing
    4. **All of the above**

417. Internet Marketing includes

    1. **Advertising**
    2. Interactive Marketing
    3. E-mail Marketing and Web advertising
    4. Display Advertising

418. The marketing manager have to carry out their responsibilities integrating all these factors in the management

1. **Process**
2. Objective
3. Goals
4. Opportunity

419. Marketing Process involves

    1. Product
    2. Demand Flow
    3. Human Needs
    4. **All of the above**

420. Advertising does appear to be important in

    1. Brand image
    2. Highlighting Specific Features
    3. Information
    4. **All of the above**

421. Which of the following is not controllable variable of marketing management ?

    1. Competitive Environment
    2. Technological Environment
    3. Science Environment
    4. **Economic Environment**

422. Which one of the following is controllable variable of marketing management ?

    1. Packaging
    2. Legal Environment
    3. **Advertisement**
    4. Political Environment

423. "A marketing policy is a statement of conter of action which will be followed under a given set of circumslances". Who said it ?

1. **William Stanton**
2. Mc Carthy
3. Manson and Rath
4. None of these

424. The marketing plan provides both

1. The vision and the cost
2. **The vision and the direction**
3. The vision and control
4. The vision and the post

425. Marketing is

1. **Essential an operational and purposive pursuit**
2. A cost of service
3. A cost of product
4. An expenses

426. Sales Promotion includes

1. Publicity
2. Sales Promotion and Personal Selling
3. Advertising
4. **All of the above**

427. Promotional mix is the particular combination of promotional tools used by a company to …….. with its audiences

1. **Communicate**
2. Help
3. Purchasing Decision
4. Plan

428. A Product line is a group of Products that are closely related to

1. **Product**
2. Promotion

3. Production style and Brand
4. Power

429. The concept of online marketing is different from concept of

1. e-commerce
2. e-Accounting
3. Commerce
4. **All of the above**

430. Which of the following point is responsiblility for effective market segmentation ?

1. Measurability
2. Easy & accessibility
3. Substantiality
4. **All of the above**

431. The Market environment consists

1. Socio-economic
2. Technology
3. Competition
4. **All of the above**

432. The life cycle concept places particular emphasis on risks. For management in any firm, of   failing to cultivate invention and innovation this statement refers to

1. Product Cost Plan
2. Market Segmentation
3. **Product Life Cycle**
4. Product Price Policy

433. Which is the basic form of Innovation ?

1. Introduction of novel production process
2. Improvement and development of existing process

3. Improvement and development of existing firm
4. All of the above

434. Co-operative societies Act was passed in

1. 1904
2. 1912
3. 1932
4. 1948
5. 2001

435. Marketing is best defined as :

1. Matching a product with its market
2. Promoting and selling products
3. Facilitating satisfying exchange relationships
4. Distributing products at the right price to stores
5. None of these

436. 'The expansion of the definition of marketing to include non business activities adds which one of these examples to the field of marketing' ?

1. Proctor and Gamble selling toothpaste
2. St. Pauls Church attracting new members
3. PepsiCo selling soft drinks
4. Liver's donating Rs. 5 to a charity with every pack purchased
5. None of these

437. Tom goes to vending machine deposits Rs. 20, and receives a Cola. Which one of the following aspects of the definition of marketing is focused on here ?

1. Production concept
2. Satisfaction of organizational goals
3. Product pricing and distribution
4. Exchange

5. None of these

438. The marketing environment is Best described as being :

   1. Composed of controllable variables
   2. Composed of variables independent of one another
   3. An indirect influence on marketing activity
   4. Dynamic and changing
   5. None of these

439. A physical, concrete product you can touch is :

   1. A service
   2. A goods
   3. An idea
   4. A concept
   5. A philosophy

440. Chimney Sweeps employs people to clean fireplaces and chimneys in homes and apartments. The firm is primarily the marketer of :

   1. A service
   2. A goods
   3. An idea
   4. An image
   5. None of these

441. Which one of the following statements by a company chairman best reflects the marketing concept ?

   1. We have organized our business to make certain that we satisfy custome's needs
   2. We believe that the marketing department must organize to sell what we produce
   3. We try to produce only high quality, technically efficient products
   4. We try to encourage company growth

5. None of these

442. The marketing concept is a way of thinking or a management philosophy that affects :

    1. Only marketing activities
    2. Most efforts of the organisation
    3. Mainly the efforts of sales personnel
    4. Mainly customer relations
    5. None of these

443. If Von Air, a hairdryer manufacturer, is focusing on customer satisfaction, it will find that what consumers really want is;

    1. More watts
    2. More speed
    3. Higher heat settings
    4. Attractive hair

444. Match the following

List – I		List – II
(Thinkers)		(Contribution)
1. Mason and Rath	(i)	Marketing and Distribution
2. Condiff and still	(ii)	Basic Marketing
3. William	(iii)	fundamental of Marketing
4. James Stephenson	(iv)	Principles and Practice of Commerce
	(v)	Costing

Codes :

	(a)	(b)	(c)	(d)
1.	1	2	4	3
2.	**1**	**2**	**3**	**4**
3.	2	1	3	4
4.	3	1	2	4

445. Match the following

List – I	List – II
(Element of Marketing)	(features)

1. Place (Distribution)   (i) Warehouse
2. Promotion   (ii) Publicity
3. Price   (iii) Margins
4. Product Quality   (iv) Durability
                          (v) Marketing Mix

Codes :

	(a)	(b)	(c)	(d)
1.	2	4	3	1
2.	3	1	4	2
3.	**1**	**2**	**3**	**4**
4.	1	3	2	4

446. Assertion (A) : Selling is important not merely for increasing the profits of businessmen, but also for making goods and services available to the consumers in society.

Reason (R) : It is the process whereby goods and services finally flow to the consumers who need them and the firm performs its functions of distributing its products among consumers.

Codes :

1. (A) and (R) both are true
2. (A) is true but (R) is not true
3. (A) is not true But (R) is true
4. **(A) and (R) are true and (R) is the reason of (A)**

447. Assertion (A) : Marketing occupies an important position in the organization.

Reason (R) : Marketing is the function of business concerned with creation of a consumer.

Codes :

1. **(A) and (R) both are true**
2. (A) is true but (R) is not true
3. (A) is not true but (R) is true
4. (A) and (R) both are untrue

448. Marketing research does not normally

1. Gather environmental information
2. **Provide a continuous source of informations**
3. Relate to all aspect of marketing operations
4. Describe the current situation

449. Marketing planning is concerned with

1. Planning the amount the placement of newspaper ads
2. Planning consignment sales contracts to be offered
3. Planning sales force size and deployment
4. **All of the above**

450. MRP stands for

1. Management Resource Planning
2. Marketing Research Planning
3. **Manufacturing Resource Planning**

4. Material Requirements Planning

451. Marketing research data is gathered by

1. Observation
2. In-depth interviews
3. Controlled experiment
4. **All of the above**

452. The most structured marketing problems are likely to be those dealing with

1. Product
2. Promotion
3. **Place**
4. Price

453. A marketing plan is composed of three basic components namely

1. Objective
2. Procedure
3. Policies
4. Decision
5. Programme
6. Command

Codes :

1. i, ii, iii
2. **i, ii, v**
3. i, v, vi
4. i, iii, iv

454. The market process involves which functions

1. Buying
2. Storing
3. Grading

4. Risk hearing
5. Transporting
6. Financing
7. Selling

Codes :

1. i, ii, v and vii
2. i, iv, v and vii
3. i, ii, iii, v, vi and vii
4. All of the above

455. Philosophy of marketing

1. Product oriented marketing
2. Production oriented marketing
3. Sale oriented marketing
4. Customer oriented marketing
5. Social marketing
6. Green marketing

Codes :

1. i, ii, iii and iv
2. ii, iii, iv and v
3. iii, iv, v and vi
4. All of the above

456. Micro marketing environment include

1. Suppliers
2. Consumer
3. Service provider
4. Local share holder

Codes :

1. i and ii
2. i, ii and iii
3. i, ii and iv

4. ii, iii and iv

457. Internal marketing environment includes

1. Employees
2. Markets
3. Service provider
4. Local shareholder
5. Consumer

Codes :

1. **i, ii, and iii**
2. i, iii and iv
3. ii, iii and iv
4. ii, iv and v

458. Marketing segmentations division of market into separate homogeneous group of customer on   the basis of

1. Geographical variables
2. Demographic factors
3. Psychographic factors
4. Behavioural basis

Codes :

1. i, ii and iii
2. i, ii and iv
3. ii, iii and iv
4. **All of the above**

459. Element of promotion mix

1. Personal selling
2. Sales promotion
3. Public relations
4. Direct mail
5. Trade fairs and exhibitions

6. Advertising

Codes :

1. i, ii, iii and iv
2. ii, I, iv and v
3. iii, iv, v and vi
4. **All of the above**

460. A market segment should be

1. Measurable
2. Durable
3. Sizeable
4. Accessible
5. Profitable

Codes :

1. i and v
2. ii and iii
3. i, ii and iv
4. **All of the above**

461. Stage of PLC

1. Introduction
2. Growth
3. Accessible
4. Maturity
5. Decline
6. Attitude

Codes :

1. i, ii, iii and iv
2. ii, iii, iv and v
3. **i, ii, iv and v**
4. All of the above

462. Macro marketing environment include

1. Culture
2. Politics
3. Economy
4. Society
5. Technology

Codes :

1. i, ii, ii and iv
2. ii, iii, iv and v
3. iii, iv, v and vi
4. **All of the above**

463. A method for achieving maximum market response from limited marketing resources by reorganizing differences in the response characteristics of various part of the market is known as

1. Market targeting
2. Market positioning
3. **Market segmentation**
4. Market strategy

464. Who plays their significant role in distribution of goods when they do not sell to ultimate users or consumers ?

1. Retailer
2. **Wholesaler**
3. Mediator
4. Commission agent

465. In marketing mix, which four P's are covered

1. **Product, Price, Place, Promotion**
2. Product, Price, Penetration Promotion
3. Product, Price
4. Product, Price, Positioning, Promotion

466. Which research includes all types of researchs into human motives when it refers to qualitative research designed to uncover the consumer's subconsciousness or hidden motivations?

    1. **Motivational Research**
    2. Marketing Research
    3. Managerial Research
    4. Price Research

467. False and mishandling claims vulgarity in advertisement do not match with

    1. Aggressive advertising
    2. Ethics in advertising
    3. **Mass level of advertising**
    4. Sales promotion.

468. Promotion in marketing means

    1. Passing an examination
    2. Elevation from one grade to another
    3. **Selling the products through various means**
    4. Selling the product in specific area

469. A "Prospect" means ....

    1. Company's prospectus
    2. Company's Memorandum of Association
    3. **A likely buyer**
    4. A likely seller

470. "USP" in marketing means ....

    1. Useful Sales Procedures
    2. Useful Selling Propositions
    3. Used Sales Plans
    4. **Unique Selling Propositions**

471. Motivation for sales persons can be achieved through ....

    1. High success rate of conversions
    2. Better sales incentives
    3. Continuous training and updation of knowledge
    4. Support from operation staff
    5. All of these

472. Marketing of Education Loans can be done by ....

    1. Approaching eligible students
    2. Approaching the parents
    3. Having tie-ups with Educational Institutes
    4. All of these

473. Education loans can be more effectively canvassed by ....

    1. Door-to-door campaigns
    2. E-mail contacts
    3. Diversification
    4. Tie-up with colleges

474. Product design is a function of ISBI

    1. Front office staff
    2. Back office staff
    3. Management
    4. Marketing and research team

475. A package which has a secondary usefulness after its contents have been consumed, is called

    1. Dual use package
    2. Bulk package
    3. Both (a) and (b)
    4. Consumer package

476. Good competition helps in

    1. Improved customer service
    2. Improved brand image
    3. More market share
    4. Better customer profile

477. A company's ability to perform in one or more ways that competitors cannot or wil not match   is known as it

    1. Brand image
    2. Brand positioning
    3. Competitive advantage
    4. Attribute positioning

478. The "USP" of a product denotes ....

    1. Usefulness of the product
    2. Drawbacks of the product
    3. Number of fallied products available
    4. High selling features of a product

479. The competitive position of a company can be improved by ....

    1. Increasing the selling price
    2. Ignoring competitors
    3. Increasing the cost price
    4. Understanding and fulfilling customer's needs

480. Value added services means ....

    1. Low cost products
    2. High cost products
    3. Additional services for the same cost
    4. Giving discounts

481. A good Brand can be built up by way of ....

1. Customer grievances
2. Break-down of IT support
3. Large number of products
4. **Consistent offering of good services**

482. What is the USP of saving accounts ?

    1. High rate of interest
    2. **Easy operation**
    3. Risky transactions
    4. Expensive transactions

483. The USP of a Credit Card is

    1. **Cashless operations**
    2. Only for HNIs
    3. Only for employed persons
    4. Transactions through cheque book

484. The USP of a Current Account is

    1. High profitability
    2. Liquidity
    3. Low rate of interest
    4. **Friendly features**

485. 'Value added services' implies

    1. Additional knowledge of marketing staff
    2. Service beyond normal hours
    3. **Service with extra facilities**
    4. Marketing agencies

486. The process of branding covers

    1. Giving on identify to a product
    2. Establishing the product

3. Popularizing the product
4. **All of the above**

487. Which of the following is the type of distributor's brand ?

    1. Private brand
    2. Dealer brand
    3. House brand
    4. **All of these**

488. The function of branding includes

    1. Ensuring legal right on product
    2. Price differentiation of products
    3. Sustaining brand above
    4. **All of above**

489. Which of the following can have the advantage of brand names ?

    1. Manufacturers
    2. Consumers
    3. Distributers
    4. **All of these**

490. Branding is the ………… process.

    1. Marketing
    2. **Management**
    3. Static
    4. Technical

491. When a brand name is registered and legalized, it becomes

    1. **Trademark**
    2. Brand mark
    3. Brand right

4. All of above

492. Which of the following is the type of manufacturer's brand ?

    1. National brand
    2. Regional brand
    3. Advertising brand
    4. All of above

493. A brand can be helpful for the manufacturers to

    1. Distinguish the product from other competing products
    2. Widen the work for products
    3. Create goodwill for the product
    4. All of above

494. The objectives of packaging are

    1. Identify the brand
    2. Aid product consumption
    3. Assist at home storage
    4. All of the above

495. A brand can be helpful for the distributers in

    1. Leading to large selling
    2. Reducing the price flexibility
    3. Reducing the cost of distribution
    4. All of the above

496. Multiple packaging is the practice of placing

    1. Several containers in one product
    2. Several units in one container
    3. Several boxes in one container
    4. Each unit in each container

497. Characteristics of good packaging is

   1. Convenient
   2. Interesting
   3. Attractive and protective
   4. All of the above

498. Which of the following may be known as the function of packaging ?

   1. To assemble and arrange the content
   2. To facilitate transporting and storing
   3. To enable the display of content
   4. All of the above

499. The types of packaging includes

   1. Family packaging
   2. Reuse packaging
   3. Multiple packaging
   4. All of above

500. Labelling is important for three reasons, first is promotional and second is legal. What is the third reason ?

   1. Information
   2. Branding
   3. Strategic
   4. Marketing

501. The label on a soft drink can reads 'cool and refreshing' for what reason are these words used ?

   1. To promote the product
   2. To encourage multiple purchases
   3. To satisfy legal requirements
   4. To provide information

502. Labelling is important for informational, legal and ………….. reasons.

    1. Branding
    2. Strategic
    3. Marketing
    4. **Promotional**

503. Which of the following is indicated by labeling ?

    1. Content
    2. Weight
    3. Price
    4. **All of these**

504. Product identification involves

    1. Branding
    2. Packaging
    3. Labeling
    4. **a, b and c**

505. Marketing includes

    1. Branding
    2. Packaging
    3. Standarlization and grading
    4. **All of above**

506. Grade labels identify by

    1. Letter
    2. Number
    3. Quality
    4. **a, b, c**

507. The package design of a bag of flour would most likely be criticized for being.

    1.   Well suited for multiple unit packaging
    2.   Unsafe to the user
    3.   **Functionally deficient**
    4.   Unsafe to the environment

508. Labeling is important for the international legal and ……… reasons.

    1.   Marketing
    2.   **Promotional**
    3.   Branding
    4.   Strategic

509. Which is the branding of Bank?

    1.   Fixed deposits or term deposits
    2.   Mutual fund
    3.   Personal loan
    4.   **All of these**

510. Which is factor of pricing?

    1.   Cash discount and allowances
    2.   Period of credit
    3.   Condition of period
    4.   **All of these**

511. A branding name facilitates –

    1.   Advertising
    2.   Functions as a demand stimulant
    3.   Social
    4.   **(a) and (b)**

512. What is one of the main bases of difference between brand and trade mark ?

    1. Registration
    2. Legal promotive
    3. Identification
    4. All of the above

513. A brand can be used by –

    1. All people all manufacturers
    2. 3 manufacturers
    3. 1 manufactures
    4. None of above

514. What is the scope of brand ?

    1. Narrow
    2. Wide
    3. Limited
    4. Waste

515. Packaging can be determined as

    1. To assemble the contents
    2. To arrange the contents
    3. To identify the contents
    4. The protect the contents

516. Which one of the following is one of the main functions of packaging ?

    1. To assemble the contents
    2. To identify the contents
    3. To protect the contents
    4. All of the above

517. Packaging facilities us in –

1. Transporting
2. Warehouse handling
3. Display
4. **All of the above**

518. How packaging is useful in advertising ?

   1. Provide opportunity for advertising
   2. Provide space for advertising
   3. Provide cheaper for advertising
   4. **(a), (b) and (c)**

519. What is one of the promotional functions of packaging ?

   1. Consumer Affluence
   2. Integrated Marketing
   3. Innovations Opportunities
   4. **All of the above**

520. What is one of the main contents of Label ?

   1. Name of producer
   2. Name of product
   3. **Qualities of production**
   4. All of the above

520. What is one of the types of labels ?

   1. Brand label
   2. Grade label
   3. Descriptive label
   4. **(a), (b) and (c)**

521. A brand is BEST defined as a

   1. Registered design or symbol that is displayed on the product
   2. Related group of words that describe the product

3. Name, symbol, design, or combination of these that identifies a seller's products
4. Copyrighted word(s) that give the manufacturer exclusive ownership

522. One distinguishing factor between a brand name and a brand mark is that a brand name

1. Creates customer loyalty
2. **Consists of work**
3. Identifies only one item in the product mix
4. Implies an organization's name

523. .... Brands usually require a producer to become involved in distribution, promotion and pricing decisions.

1. Retailer
2. **Manufacturer**
3. Own label
4. Wholesaler

524. When a firm uses one of its existing brand names as part of a brand name for an improved or new product, the branding is called ....

1. Individual branding
2. Overall family branding
3. Line family branding
4. **Brand extension branding**

525. A carton of orange juice has no brand name on the package, only the name of the product 'orange juice'. This is an example of

1. A manufacturer's brand
2. An own label brand
3. A no frills brand
4. **A generic brand**

526. The four levels of brands are the tangible product, the basic brand, the potential brand and the .... brand.

   1. Targeted
   2. Augmented
   3. Aggregated
   4. Positioned

527. Labeling is important for three reasons, including promotional and legal reasons. What is the third reason ?

   1. Marketing
   2. Branding
   3. Strategic
   4. Informational

528. Labeling, packaging are associated with :

   1. Price mix
   2. Product mix
   3. Place mix
   4. Promotion mix

529. The firm uses any existing brand to introduce in market a new product, the brand is classified as

   1. Brand extension
   2. Sub-brand
   3. Parent brand
   4. Product extension

530. The branding strategy is also called

   1. Brand architecture
   2. Branding rate
   3. Branding earnings
   4. Brand responsiveness

531. When the companies combine existing brand with new brands the brands is called

    1. Parent brand
    2. Product extension
    3. Brand extension
    4. Sub-brand

532. The parent brand if associated with multiple products in brand extension is called

    1. Family brand
    2. Product extension
    3. Sub-product
    4. Parent company

533. The brand which is result of extension of brand or sub-brand is classified as

    1. Brand extension
    2. Sub-brand
    3. Parent brand
    4. Product extension

534. Value added service means

    1. Costlier products
    2. Additional benefits at the same cost
    3. Extra work by the sales persons
    4. None of these

535. Setting price of a product based on the buyer's perceptions of value rather than on the seller's cost is known as

1. Break Even Pricing
2. Target Profit Pricing
3. Cost Plus Pricing
4. **Value Based Pricing**

536. Which one of the following best describes the term 'Negative Demand'?

1. Consumers begin to buy a product less frequently
2. Consumers do not at all buy a product
3. Consumers are unaware or uninterested in a product
4. **Consumers dislike a product and may even pay to avoid it**

537. Leads for canvassing home loan accounts can be obtained from :

1. **Builders**
2. Individuals building one's own house
3. Brick manufacturers
4. Cement suppliers

538. Generation of sales leads can be improved by

1. Being very talkative
2. **Increasing personal and professional contacts**
3. Being passive
4. Engaging recovery agent

539. Personal Loans can be canvassed among

1. **Salaried persons**
2. Pensioners
3. Foreign Nationals
4. NRI-customers

540. Proper pricing is needed from

1. Extra changes for extra services
2. **Good customers services**
3. Service with extra facilities
4. Putting burden on the customer

541. Of the following pricing strategies ………. is not ideal for new products.

1. Skimming products
2. **Discriminatory product**
3. Promotional pricing
4. All of these

542. Which pricing approach is used to avoid the problem of over pricing and under pricing ?

1. Cost based approach
2. Buyer based approach
3. **Competition based approach**
4. All of these

543. Which of the following is known as plastic money ?

1. Bearer cheques
2. **Credit cards**
3. Demand draft
4. Gift cheques

544. The pricing strategy for credit card depends on

1. Competition
2. **Customer's income**
3. Customer relations
4. Customer awareness

545. Setting price of a product based on the buyers perception of value rather than on the sellers cost is known as

1. Break even pricing
2. Taret profit pricing
3. Cost plus pricing
4. **Value based pricing**

546. Price is

   1. **The value that is exchanged for products in a marketing transaction**
   2. Always money paid in a marketing transaction
   3. More important to buyers than sellers
   4. Usually the most inflexible marketing mix decision variable

547. Price is a key element in the marketing mix because it relates directly to

   1. **The generation of total force**
   2. The size of an exchange
   3. The speed of an exchange
   4. Brand image

548. 'Skimming price' for the new product is called

   1. Low initial price
   2. Average price
   3. **High initial price**
   4. Moderate price

549. Under monopoly market structure the degree of freedom in pricing decision is

   1. Very low
   2. **Very high**
   3. Quite good
   4. Zero

550. A firm that practices price competition engages in which one of the following strategies ?

    1. **Beating or matching the prices of competitions**
    2. Setting prices only as low as the second lowest competitor
    3. Competing in both price and product differentiation
    4. Letting other firms cut price while it retains profitability

551. The maximum selling price that a firm can sustain for a product is determined by

    1. Competitor's prices
    2. What is cost to produce competitor's prices
    3. Competitive parity
    4. **What customers are prepared to pay for it**

552. All of the following would be considered to be among the internal factors that affect price decisions, expect.

    1. Nature of the market and demand
    2. Competition
    3. **Costs**
    4. Environmental factors such as the economy and social concepts

553. Coca-Cola carries a different price depending on whether the consumer purchases it in a fine restaurant, a fast food restaurant or in an airport. This is known as

    1. Location pricing
    2. **Channel pricing**
    3. Image pricing
    4. Customer segment pricing

554. Many restaurants observe 'Happy House' during the leave time of the day. This is known as

    1. **Time pricing**
    2. Image pricing
    3. Customer profit pricing
    4. Location pricing

555. In going rate pricing, the firm bases its price largely on .... prices.

    1. Market
    2. **Competitor's**
    3. Actual product
    4. Customer segment

556. Indian railway charges a lower fare to senior citizen's. It is an example of

    1. Product form pricing
    2. **Customer segment pricing**
    3. Image pricing
    4. Time pricing

557. What is the significance pricing has ?

    1. Social implications
    2. Physical implications
    3. Economical implications
    4. **(a) and (d)**

558. Price can be describe as .... item for consumer.

    1. **Expense**
    2. Consumption
    3. Favourable
    4. Unfavorable

559. Price can be determined as exchange value of –

    1. Consumer product
    2. Industrial product
    3. Service
    4. (a), (b) and (c)

560. What is one of the aspects which is important in pricing decisions ?

    1. Social consideration
    2. Ethical consideration
    3. Status quo objectives
    4. All of above

561. Price is very important from social point of view why ?

    1. Optimum use of material
    2. Optimum use of labour
    3. Optimum use of capital
    4. (a), (b) and (c)

562. Lesser price will

    1. Attract more customers
    2. Attract more tax
    3. Attract more competitors
    4. Attract more exports

563. What forces tend to push prices down ?

    1. Large supply
    2. Strong competition
    3. Bearish attitude
    4. All of above

564. How many pricing strategies a producer during marketing pioneering stage ?

1. One
2. **Two**
3. Four
4. Nine

565. Name the pricing policy, a producer has during marketing pioneering stage ?

1. Price Skimming
2. Price maker
3. Penetration pricing strategy
4. **(a) and (c)**

566. In which pricing strategy producer set a high introductory price for their product ?

1. Penetration pricing strategy
2. Price taker
3. Single price policy
4. **Price skimming**

567. Pricing policy provides

1. Guideline with in which pricing strategy is formulated
2. Guideline with in which pricing strategy is implemented
3. Low price policy
4. **(a) and (b)**

568. Under which pricing policy, prices are fixed in such a way that they have some kind a way that they have some kind of psychological influence on the buyer ?

1. Laeder pricng
2. Keep out pricing
3. Skimming the cream price
4. **Psychological pricing**

569. Which type of pricing is commonly found in the retail trade ?

1. **Mark up pricing**
2. Competitive pricing
3. Follow the leader pricing
4. Resale price maintenance

570. Which type of pricing policy emphasis to a specified return on selling of product ?

1. **Target pricing**
2. Mark up pricing
3. Competitive pricing
4. Going rate pricing

571. The practice of charging different prices from different customers is called –

1. **Price Discriminations**
2. Price Fluctuation
3. Price Variable
4. Price stable

572. Which of the following is one of the types of price discrimination ?

1. Personal price discrimination
2. Geographical price discrimination
3. Time price discrimination
4. **All of above**

573. In which system prices are being charged as per the classes of consumers ?

1. **Class price discrimination**
2. Time price discrimination
3. Personal price discrimination
4. Geographical price discrimination

574. It is a method in which various products are combined at the same price :

1. Promotional pricing
2. **Product bundle pricing**
3. Captive product pricing
4. Optimal product pricing

575. Differentiation in pricing for various geographical customer

1. Price skimming
2. Psychological pricing
3. Pricing variations
4. **Geographical pricing**

576. The pricing strategy used to set prices of the products that are must be used with the main product is called

1. Optimal product pricing
2. **Product line pricing**
3. Competitive pricing
4. Captive product pricing

577. The new product pricing strategy through which the companies set lower prices to gain large market share is classified as

1. Optimal product pricing
2. Skimming pricing
3. **Penetration pricing**
4. Captive product pricing

578. The pricing strategy in which prices are set lower to actual price to trigger short term sales is classified as

    1. **Promotional pricing**
    2. Short term pricing
    3. Quick pricing
    4. Cyclical pricing

579. The pricing strategy in which company divides location into different sectors and charge same price for each sector is classified as

    1. Freight on board origin pricing
    2. **Zone pricing**
    3. Basing point pricing
    4. Uniform delivered pricing

580. The kind of reduction made to those buyers who buy large volumes of products is classified as

    1. Cash discount
    2. Seasonal discount
    3. Functional discount
    4. **Quantity discount**

581. Public relations is

    1. Part of customer service
    2. Part of marketing
    3. Part of image building
    4. **All of these**

582. Team building is required

    1. Only for lead generation
    2. Only for after sales service
    3. **For cross selling**

4. All of above

583. The performance of a salesperson can be enhanced by

1. Increasing the sales incentives
2. Increasing the number of products to be sold
3. Appropriate training
4. **All of above**

584. Source of sales leads are

1. Data mining
2. Media outlets
3. Promotional programs
4. **All of above**

585. Advertisement is a type of

1. **Direct marketing**
2. Service marketing
3. Indirect marketing
4. Internal marketing

586. Effective selling skills depend on

1. Good dress sense
2. Territory allocation
3. Sales call planning
4. **Good eye contact**

587. The performance of a sales person depends on

1. **Ability and willingness of the sales person**
2. Incentive paid
3. Size of the sales team
4. Team leader's attitude

588. Mass communication with customers potential customers, usually through paid public media is known as

1. Publicity
2. Sales promotion
3. **Advertising**
4. Brand building

589. Find the incorrect option. It sales promotion involves

1. Building product awareness
2. Creating interest
3. **Providing information**
4. Designing new products

590. Effective selling skills depends on

1. Size of the sales team
2. Age of the sales team
3. **Knowledge level of the sales team**
4. Educational level of the sales team

591. A direct selling agent (DSA) is required to be adept in ………….

1. Surrogate marketing
2. Training skills
3. **Communication skills**
4. OTC marketing

592. Effective selling skills depends on ………..

1. Number of languages known to the DSA
2. Data on marketing staff
3. Information regarding IT market
4. **Knowledge to related markets**

593. A successful marketing person requires one of the following qualities ....

    1. **Empathy**
    2. Sympathy
    3. Insistence
    4. Aggressiveness

594. Good public relations indicate

    1. Improved marketing skills
    2. Improved brand image
    3. Improved customer service
    4. **All of above**

595. Advertisements are required for

    1. Boosting the production levels
    2. Motivating the employees
    3. **Boosting the above**
    4. All of above

596. Advertising is a major promotion mix ingredient that is a

    1. Non-paid form of non-personal communication
    2. Paid form of personal communication
    3. Paid form of non-personal communication
    4. **None of the above**

597. Which of the following is a means of advertising ?

    1. Cinema
    2. Demonstration
    3. Radio and television
    4. **All of these**

598. Which of the following is the drawback of advertising ?

1. Wastage of money
2. Reduction of ethics
3. Mis-representation of facts
4. **All of above**

599. Which is a type of advertising ?

1. Direct advertising
2. Indirect action advertising
3. Primary demand advertising
4. **All of above**

600. The major stages of advertising development include

1. Domestic
2. Export
3. International
4. **Multinational and global**

601. Online advertising uses

1. Internet
2. World wide web
3. **Both (a) and (b)**
4. Radio

602. What is a product ?

a. Goods which are produced for the sale purpose of consumption

b. **Anything that satisfies consumers wants or needs and involves transfer of title**

c. Anything that satisfies a need or want and can be offered on the market for attention, acquisition use or consumption, including physical objects, services, organizations ideas and mixes of the above

d. Any physical good

603. **Statement I :** The firm should "stick to its niching" but not necessarily to its niche.

Statement II : Multiple niching is not preferable to single niching.

Codes :
- a. Both the Statements are true.
- b. Both the Statements are false.
- **c. Statement I is true, but Statement II is false.**
- d. Statement II is true, but Statement I is false.

604. A descriptive thought that a person holds about something is called

- **a.** **Belief**
- b. Learning
- c. Attitude
- d. Perception

605. The concept of achieving maximum profits through increased consumer satisfaction for raised market share focuses on

- a. Product
- b. Selling
- **c.** **Customer**
- d. Production

606. Match the following items of List-I (sources of competition) with List-II (examples for these sources of competition) and indicate the code of correct matching.

List – I

- a. Directly similar products
- b. Available substitutes
- c. Unrelated products

List - II

- a. OLA Taxi and Metro Rail
- b. Mercedes and BMW

c. PVR and Amusement park

Codes

	(A)	(B)	(C)
d.	iii	ii	i
e.	i	iii	ii
f.	i	ii	iii
g.	ii	i	iii

607. The marketing task which finds ways to alter the time pattern of demand through flexible pricing, promotion and other incentives is called

    h. Demarketing
    i. Synchromarketing
    j. Fleximarketing
    k. Gorilla Marketing

608. Which of the following is not a reason for a firm to lose its market share to competitors?

a. **A product/model is perceived by the target customer group as satisfying needs.**
b. Customers not being covered by the company's sales force and distribution outlets.
c. Customers may have been lost to competitors due to poor service by the firm or its sales personnel or product becoming obsolete or more expensive.
d. All the above are correct reasons for given condition.

609. Match the items of List-I with List-II and denote the code of correct matching.

List - I

a. Invest Strategy
b. Protect Strategy
c. Harvest Strategy

d. Divest   Strategy

List – II

a. No receiving of new resources.
b. Well financed marketing efforts.
c. Selective resource allocation
d. Not warranting substantial new resources.

Codes :

	A	B	C	D
a.	**ii**	**iii**	**iv**	**i**
b.	i	iii	ii	iv
c.	ii	i	iv	iii
d.	iv	iii	ii	i

610. An elaborated version of the idea expressed in meaningful consumer term is called

a. Product image
b. Product idea
c. **Product concept**
d. Prototype

611. Which of the following requires consumers to interpret ambiguous stimuli?

a. Focus group method
b. **Projective techniques**
c. Rejective techniques
d. Semantic differential scales

612. Which of the following passes through the four stages of distinctiveness, emulation, mass fashion and decline ?

1. Style
2. **Fashion**
3. Fad

4. Style and Fashion

613. Which of the following positioning strategies is adopted by marketers to position their product in two categories simultaneously ?

    1.   Point of Difference
    2.   Point of Parity
    3.   **Straddle Positioning**
    4.   Emotional Positioning

614. **Statement (I)** : Marketing is the process by which a firm profitably translates customer needs into revenue.
Statement (II) : Marketing is the messages and/or actions that causes messages and/or actions.
Codes :
    1.   (I) is correct but (II) is not correct.
    2.   (II) is correct but (I) is not correct.
    3.   **(I) and (II) both are correct.**
    4.   (I) and (II) both are incorrect.

615. **Assertion (A)** : Odd pricing aims at maximising profit by making micro-adjustments in pricing structure.
Reasoning (R) : Odd pricing refers to a price ending in 1, 3, 5, 7, or 9. When examining a price, the first digits carry more weight than the last ones.
Codes :
    1.   (A) is right and (R) is wrong.
    2.   (A) is wrong and (R) is right.
    3.   **Both (A) and (R) are right.**
    4.   Both (A) and (R) are wrong.

616. Name the process in which a buyer posts its interest in buying a certain quantity of item and sellers compete for the business by submitting lower bid until there is only one seller left.

    a.   Internet
    b.   **Reverse auction**
    c.   B2B market place
    d.   B2C market place

617. A Product line is a group of Products that are closely related to

a. **Product**
b. Promotion
c. Production style and Brand
d. Power

618. The concept of online marketing is different from concept of

a. e-commerce
b. e-Accounting
c. Commerce
d. **All of the above**

619. Which of the following point is responsiblility for effective market segmentation ?

a. Measurability
b. Easy & accessibility
c. Substantiality
d. **All of the above**

620. The Market environment consists

a. Socio-economic
b. Technology
c. Competition
d. **All of the above**

621. The life cycle concept places particular emphasis on risks. For management in any firm, of failing to cultivate invention and innovation this statement refers to

a. Product Cost Plan
b. Market Segmentation
c. **Product Life Cycle**
d. Product Price Policy

622. Which is the basic form of Innovation ?

a. Introduction of novel production process
b. Improvement and development of existing process
c. Improvement and development of existing firm
d. All of the above

623. Co-operative societies Act was passed in

a. 1904
b. 1912
c. 1932
d. 1948

624. Marketing is best defined as :

a. Matching a product with its market
b. Promoting and selling products
c. Facilitating satisfying exchange relationships
d. Distributing products at the right price to stores

625. Advertising method in which an advertisement is broadcasted simultaneously on several radio stations and / or television channels is known as

a. Black-out
b. Consolidation
c. Road-block
d. Cornering

626. Which type of differentiation is used to gain competitive advantage through the way a firm designs its distribution coverage, expertise and performance ?

a. Channel differentiation
b. Services differentiation
c. People differentiation

d. Product differentiation

627. Which one of the following is the most likely result of a marketing strategy that attempts to serve all potential customers ?
1. All customers will be delighted.
2. Customer-perceived value will be increased.
3. The company will need to follow up with a demarketing campaign.
4. **Not all customers will be satisfied.**

628. Which of the following is not a primary activity in Michael Porter's value chain ?

a. Inbound logistics
b. Operations
c. Outbound logistics
d. **Procurement**

629. Which of the following represents consistency of results when the test instrument is used repeatedly ?

e. Validity
f. **Reliability**
g. Relativity
h. Sensitivity

630. **Assertion (A)** : Too many stimuli make a person accommodated to those sensations. Sensory adaptation is a problem that concerns many advertisers, which is why they try to change their advertising campaigns regularly.
Reason (R) : To cut through advertising clutter and to ensure that consumers perceive advertisement, marketers try to increase sensory input.
Codes :
a. (A) is right and (R) is wrong.
b. (A) is wrong and (R) is right.
c. Both (A) and (R) are right but (R) does not explain (A).
d. Both (A) and (R) are right and (R) explains (A).

631. The three levels of product are –

a. Raw, Semi finished & finished

b. Core product, Actual product and Augmented promotion

c. Price, place, Promotion

d. Tangible Product, Services ideas

632. Which of the following researches is meant to study deferent aspects of sale in an enterprises ?

1. Research on sales markets and policies
2. Research on customer and policies
3. A research on sales advertisement and policies
4. **Research on sales methods and policies**

633. Match the following

List – I (Functions of Marketing Process)	List – II (Area)
5. Functions of Exchange	(i) Selling
6. Transfer of Ownership	(ii) Buying and Selling
7. Functions of Transportations	(iii)
8. Facilitating Functions	(iv) Financing
	(v) Costing

Codes :
(a) (b) (c) (d)

	1	2	3	4
9.	1	2	3	4
10.	4	2	3	1
11.	3	1	2	4
12.	2	3	1	4

634. Match the following

List – I		List – II	
(P's of Marketing)		(Elements)	
1.	Product	(i)	Warranty
2.	Price Facility	(ii)	Credit
3.	Promotion Selling	(iii)	Personal
4.	Place Location (Distribution)	(iv)	Factory
		(v)	Marketing

Codes :

	(a)	(b)	(c)	(d)
1.	1	2	3	4
2.	4	3	2	1
3.	3	1	2	4
4.	2	1	3	4

635. Match the following

List – I		List – II	
(Bases of Segmenting Industrial Market)		(Factors)	
1.	Physical Industry	(i)	Size of
2.	Operational Policy	(ii)	Logistic

3. Purchases	(iii) Lobby Status
4. Situational Order	(iv) Specific
	(v) Risk Factor

Codes :

	(a)	(b)	(c)	(d)
1.	**1**	**2**	**3**	**4**
2.	4	5	1	2
3.	2	3	1	4
4.	4	5	1	2

636. Match the following

List – I

(Marketing Sub-plans)

1. Base Line
2. Research
3. Technical Plan
4. Organizational Plan
5. Contingency Plan Expansion

List – II

(Factors)

(i) Market
(ii) Segmentation
(iii) Branding
(iv) Distribution
(v) Market
(vi) Tax

Codes :

	(a)	(b)	(c)	(d)
1.	2	3	4	1
2.	**1**	**2**	**3**	**4**
3.	1	3	2	4
4.	1	2	4	3

637. Match the following

List – I

(Marketing Sub-plans)

List – II

(Variables)

1.	Baseline Research Service	(i)	Customer
2.	Technical Plan	(ii)	Packaging
3.	Organisational Plan	(iii)	Regulation
4.	Contingency Plan Management	(iv)	Risk
		(v)	Tax

Codes :

	(a)	(b)	(c)	(d)
1.	1	2	3	4
2.	2	3	1	4
3.	1	3	2	4
4.	4	2	3	1

638. Match the following

	List – I		List – II
	(Authors)		(Ideas)
1.	Bill Bishop Marketing for the Digital Age	(i)	Strategic
2.	D Bird Commonsense Direct Marketing	(ii)	
3.	Daniel S. Jonal Marketing	(iii)	Online
4.	Jeffery F. Rayport the Market space	(iv)	Managing is
		(v)	e-commerce

Codes :

	(a)	(b)	(c)	(d)
1.	1	2	3	4
2.	5	1	4	3
3.	3	1	2	4
4.	3	2	4	1

639. Match the following

	List – I (Product on the Basis of Psychology)		List – II (Examples)
1.	Pestige Products	(i)	Ownership on the Car
2.	Maturity Products	(ii)	Cold drink
3.	Anxiety Products	(iii)	Swap
4.	Hedonic Products	(iv)	Biscuit and Bread
		(v)	Firm

Codes :

	(a)	(b)	(c)	(d)
1.	**1**	**2**	**3**	**4**
2.	4	3	1	2
3.	1	2	4	3
4.	2	1	3	4

640. If market research shows that aggregate of people do not desire a particular product, the people in that aggregate;

1. Are a market for the product
2. Do not have the ability to purchase the product
3. **Are not a market for the product**
4. Are a market but will not purchase the product.

641. Which of the following is an example of a customer in an organizational market?

1. A homemaker who buys detergent
2. A customer who hires a solicitor

3. A shop owner who buys pencils for use in his shop
4. **A plant manager who buys petrol for his car**

642. The two approaches to identify a target market are;

1. Total market and undifferentiated approaches
2. Product differentiation and customer differentiation approaches
3. Multisegment and concentration approach
4. **Total market and market segmentation approach**

643. **Statement(I):** Designing a distribution system for a service (for-profit or non-business context) involves to select the parties only through which ownership will pass.
   Statement(II): The ownership channel for most of the services is long and quite complex because of inseparability characteristic.
   Statement(III): Short channel susually mean more control on the part of the seller.

   Identify the correct code of being the statements correct or incorrect. These statements relate to channel strategies of products /services.
   1. Statements (I) and (II) are correct but (III) is not correct.
   2. Statements (I) and (III)are correct but (II) is not correct.
   3. **Statements (I) and (II) are not correct but (III) is correct.**
   4. Statements (I),(II) and (III) all are not correct.

644. An enormous collection of data on various topics from a variety of internal and external sources, compiled by a firm for its own use or for use by its clients, is called:

   a. Data-base   b. **Data warehouse**

   c. Data mining   d. M.I.S.

645. Decision making involves the choice of a course of action is –

   1. Achieve success

2. Achieve sale Target
3. **Achieve pre Determined objectives**
4. Achieve incentive targets

646. Which of the following is means of outdoor advertising ?

1. Sandwich board advertising
2. Electric display
3. Posters
4. **All of above**

647. Promotional advertising includes

1. Showroom and exhibition
2. Window advertising
3. Interior display
4. **All of above**

648. Advertising is a form of …………….. intended to persuade an audience to purchase a product of service.

1. **Communication**
2. Sales
3. Market planning
4. Both (a) and (b)

649. The outdoor advertising include

1. Wall display
2. Vehicular display
3. Billboard display
4. **All of these**

650. Advertising is a form of paid non-personal presentation of ideas, goods or services for the purpose of

1. Brand
2. Newspaper
3. Advertisement
4. **Inducing people to buy**

651. The client of an advertising agency is called

    1. **Customer**
    2. Corporate
    3. Account
    4. All of these

652. Mail advertising includes

    1. Booklets
    2. Novelty gift
    3. Business reply envelope
    4. **All of above**

653. The function of advertising involves

    1. To introduce new products
    2. To explain causes of shortages
    3. All of above
    4. **None of above**

654. Which of the following is the means of bank advertising ?

    1. Newspaper or magazine
    2. Poster
    3. Television
    4. **All of the above**

655. Which is the element of advertising ?

    1. Public presentation
    2. Non-personal process

3. Written or printed in words
4. **All of the above**

656. The advertising process may be classified as

1. Product advertising
2. Pioneering advertising
3. Institutional advertising
4. **All of the above**

657. Direct mail advertising includes

1. Post card
2. Booklets
3. Price list
4. **All of these**

658. The five Ms of advertising are mission, money, message, media and

1. Marketing
2. Market share
3. **Measurement**
4. All of these

659. What is the main purpose of sales promotion ?

1. Encourage consumer to buy the product
2. Persuade consumer to buy the product
3. Premium product, free sample distribution
4. **(a) and (b)**

660. What is the main object of sales promotion ?

1. To introduce new product
2. To attract new customers
3. To face the competition

4. (a), (b) and (c)

661. What is the main advantage of sales promotion ?

1. **Helps in creating demand**
2. Cheating
3. Black marketing
4. Increase in corruption

662. The parties who has got advantages through sales promotion is called

1. Manufactures
2. Middleman
3. Wholesalers
4. (a) and (c)

663. What is the advantage manufacturer has out of sales promotion ?

1. Helps in creating demand for new product
2. Helps in getting new customers
3. Helps in minimizing the cost
4. (a), (b) and (c)

664. What is the advantage of sales promotion to middleman ?

1. Helps in selling the product
2. Helps in increasing the profit
3. Increase the goodwill
4. **All of above**

665. What is the advantage of sales promotion to consumers ?

1. Source of Eduation
2. Schemes and discounts
3. Information about the new products
4. **All of above**

666. What is one of the methods of sales promotion ?

   1. Consumer promotion method
   2. Dealer promotion method
   3. Competitor method
   4. **(a) and (b)**

667. Dealer promotion method includes

   1. Advertisement Allowance
   2. Quantity discount
   3. Incentives to salesman
   4. **All of above**

668. What are the main limitations of sales promotion ?

   1. Focus on short term aspect
   2. Sales promotion alone is useless
   3. Not helpful in removing the drawbacks of advertisement programme
   4. **All of above**

669. Which of the following is not a likely outcome to sales promotion activities ?

   1. Getting customers to "load up" on product
   2. **Long term consumer loyalty**
   3. Including consumers to try a new launch
   4. Promotes brand

670. Is sales promotion the different concept than personal selling ?

   1. True in perfect competition
   2. False in monopoly
   3. False
   4. **True**

671. Direct marketing means

    1. Advertisements
    2. Banners
    3. Face to face selling
    4. Achieving targets

672. Selling process includes

    1. Publicity
    2. Lead generation
    3. Cross-country contacts
    4. Product designing

673. Cross selling means

    1. City to city sales
    2. Selling with cross face
    3. Selling with crossed finger
    4. Selling products to existing customers

674. Full form of DSA is ………..

    1. Delivery Staff Agency
    2. Direct Selling Agent
    3. Direct Supplier Agent
    4. Distribution & Supply Agency

675. Motivating customers to buy upgraded products when they had intended to buy something of lower value is known as :

    1. Cross selling
    2. Forward selling
    3. Channel marketing
    4. Up selling

676. The concept of selling is different from marketing and aims at profit maximization through

    1. **Increasing sales volume of quality products**
    2. Customer satisfaction
    3. Satisfaction of customer needs
    4. Innovation and market research

677. Relationship marketing is useful for

    1. Trade between relatives
    2. Trade between sister concerns
    3. **Cross-selling of selling of products**
    4. Preparing a list of relatives

678. Source of sales leads are

    1. Market research
    2. Market outlets
    3. Promotional programs
    4. **All of above**

679. A call in marketing means

    1. To phone the customers
    2. To visit the customers
    3. To visit the marketing site
    4. **To call on prospective customers**

680. After sales service is not the job of

    1. Marketing staff
    2. **Sales persons**
    3. Directors of the company
    4. Employees of the company

681. What is the nature of Advertisement ?

1. **Repeatitive**
2. Irregular
3. Regular
4. Distinctive

682. Sales promotion is of ………….. nature.

1. **Irregular**
2. Distinctive
3. Repeatitive
4. Regular

683. Business enterprises has …………. Control on sales promotion.

1. Little
2. **Greater**
3. Simple
4. Effective

684. What is the base of difference between sales, advertising and personal selling ?

1. Nature
2. Necessity
3. Scope
4. **All of above**

685. Which of the following is a method of sales promotion ?

1. Free gifts to consumers
2. Discount coupons
3. Premium product
4. **All of above**

686. What is one of the advantages of advertisement to consumers ?

1. Knowledge of new product
2. Convenient purchasing
3. Saving to time
4. **(a), (b) and (c)**

687. What is the advantage of advertisement society has ?

1. Employment opportunity
2. Increase in standard of living
3. Encouragement to healthy competition
4. **All of above**

688. Advertisement provides knowledge of new products and commodities to the society to

1. Increase in sale
2. Increase in fraud
3. **Increase in standard of living**
4. Education

689. Newspapers are sold for very cheaper rates because

1. It contains discount coupon
2. It is used for criminal activities
3. **It contains advertisement**
4. It enjoys subsidy

690. Through advertisement consumers used to take their purchasing decision in advance. In this way advertisement helps in

1. **Convenient purchasing**
2. Purchase parity
3. Purchase return
4. Social obligation

691. Which advertisement media will you prefer for immediate effect of it ?

1. News paper
2. Radio
3. Posters
4. **(a), (c) and (d)**

692. Which advertisement media is suitable for long lasting effect of advertisement ?

1. Television
2. Radio
3. **Magazine**
4. News papers

693. Which of the following is a mode of advertisements ?

1. Press advertisement
2. Outdoor advertisement
3. Mail advertisement
4. **All of above**

694. What is one of the types of press advertisement ?

1. News paper
2. Magazines
3. Directories
4. **All of above**

695. Which of the following is a mode of outdoor advertisement ?

1. Sign boards
2. Sandwich advertisement
3. Transport advertisement
4. **None of above**

696. Advertisements which comes under the category of entertainment advertisement is

1. Cinema
2. Radio
3. Exhibitions
4. **All of above**

697. A type of mail advertisement is

1. Sale bill
2. Magazines
3. Catalogue
4. **(b) and (c)**

698. In a selling process in today's world

1. Only standard products are sold
2. No customization required
3. The seller need not have product knowledge
4. **The seller should aim at customer satisfaction**

699. Relationship marketing means

1. Selling to relatives
2. Selling by relatives
3. **After sales service**
4. Cross selling

700. Direct marketing means ....

1. Face to face marketing
2. Over the counter marketing
3. **Door to door marketing**
4. All of above

701. Direct mail advertising is suitable for

1. **Share brocker**
2. Hotel
3. Doctor
4. Manufacturer

702. The performance of actual selling activity is called

1. **Personal selling**
2. Sales promotion
3. Sales campaign
4. All of above

703. Which is an activity of personal selling ?

1. **To sell the product to consumer directly**
2. To train the sales force
3. To maintain the sales records
4. (a), (b) and (c)

704. "Sales promotion programme or measures are not helpful in improving the product." It is a .... of sale promotion.

1. Advantage
2. **Limitation**
3. Adverse effect
4. Punctualness

705. Who said "Personal selling consists of contacting prospective buyers of product personally" ?

1. **Richard Buskirk**
2. William J. Stanton
3. Marshal
4. Robinson

706. The concept in which sellers and buyers come in direct contact with each other, is called ......

1. **Personal selling**
2. Selling
3. Window shopping
4. Shopping

707. Which selling method is the oldest method of selling products ?

1. Counter
2. **Personal selling**
3. Further selling
4. Selling

708. Which is the function of personal selling ?

1. To cheat customers
2. **To remove doubts and confusions of customers**
3. To sell inferior product
4. To charge more price

709. What is one of the advantages of personal selling ?

1. Helpful in getting new customers
2. Helpful in demon strating product
3. Helpful in communication
4. **All of above**

710. Increase in the cost of sale is the .... of personal selling.

1. Advantage
2. **Limitation**
3. Capital
4. Costing

711. Selling is totally depends upon the :

1. Ability of salesman
2. Capability of salesman
3. Experience of salesman
4. **All of above**

712. Personal selling is responsible for

    1. Creating demand
    2. Increasing demand
    3. Maintaining demand
    4. **(a), (b) and (c)**

713. Personal selling is of ……….. nature.

    1. **Regular**
    2. Irregular
    3. Necessary
    4. Scope

714. Personal selling is ……….

    1. Necessary
    2. Unnecessary
    3. **Not so necessary**
    4. Always problematic

715. Scope of personal selling is ………..

    1. Narrow
    2. **Most narrow**
    3. Wider
    4. Widest

716. publicity may be

    1. Oral
    2. Written
    3. Personal and non-personal

4. All of above

717. Word-of-mouth marketing is

1. Triggered by the company
2. **Unpaid advertising**
3. Used by the company to influence behavior
4. All of the above

718. A paid form of non-personal communication about an organization and its products that is transmitted a target audience through a mass medium is

1. **Advertising**
2. Publicity
3. Personal selling
4. Sales promotion

719. Which of the following is considered to be any paid form of non-personal and promotion of ideas, goods or services by an identified sponsor ?

a. Personal selling
b. **Advertising**
c. Direct marketing
d. Sales promotion

720. Which of the following may have favourable or unfavourable impression on the public about the company and its products ?

1. **Publicity**
2. Advertising
3. Promotion
4. Forecasting

721. Direct marketing is necessary for

1. Having a focused approach
2. Boosting sales
3. Better customer contracts
4. **All of above**

722. Direct marketing is useful for ……….

1. Designing products
2. Sending e-mails
3. Increased production
4. **Bigger job opportunities**

723. Direct marketing is useful for

1. Designing products
2. Increased production
3. Increased opportunities
4. **None of these**

724. In the personal selling process, ……….. and ………. are involved.

1. Producer, seller
2. Buyer, producer
3. Retailer, wholesaler
4. **Seller, buyer**

725. Personal selling facilitates the process of

1. Production
2. Distribution
3. Consumption
4. **All of the above**

726. The effectiveness of personal selling depends upon

1. Qualities of product

2. Suitable price of product
3. Qualities of customers
4. **Qualities of salesman**

727. Merit of personal selling includes

1. Pinpoints prospects
2. Helps close the sale
3. Demonstrates the product
4. **All of the above**

728. Marketing and selling are

1. Not required if profit is high
2. Not required if sales are high
3. Not required in monopolistic conditions
4. **None of these**

729. Personal selling is a .... communication.

1. One way
2. **Two way**
3. Single way
4. Many to one way

730. The importance of personal selling includes

1. Benefits to consumers
2. Benefits to business
3. Benefits to society
4. **All of above**

731. Which of the following is / are the feature of personal selling ?

1. Use fewer resources
2. Contract between buyer and seller after the sale
3. Purchases tend to involve large sums of money

4. All of above

732. Personal selling involves ………… interaction of salesman with the individuals.

1. **Direct**
2. Indirect
3. Instant
4. Close

733. Personal selling consist of

1. Personal communication and advertising
2. Individual relation
3. Sales promotion
4. **None of above**

734. Personal selling is confined to a

1. **Particular area**
2. Large number of people
3. Complete area
4. Random area

735. Which of the following includes the stage of personal selling ?

1. Prospecting
2. Making first contact
3. Objection handling
4. **All of above**

736. The personal selling aims at selling ……. Products.

1. Declining
2. **Existing**
3. Inferior
4. Worthless

737. Where under a contract of sale the transfer of property in goods is to take place at a future time or subject to some condition thereafter to be fulfilled, the contract is called

   1. A sale
   2. Gift
   3. **Agreement to sell**
   4. Contract to transfer of property

738. The meaning of digital marketing is

   1. Selling digital goods
   2. Selling calculators
   3. **Selling through internet**
   4. All of these

739. Telemarketing involves –

   1. **Good communication skills**
   2. High level of motivation
   3. Door-to-door campaigns
   4. Event management

740. Online marketing is –

   1. Same as face-to-face marketing
   2. **Easier than traditional marketing**
   3. Boring as customers are not visible
   4. Voluminous task

741. Internet marketing means –

   1. Marketing to onself
   2. Marketing to the core group
   3. Marketing to the employees
   4. **None of these**

742. Online marketing is mostly useful for marketing of

1. Saving accounts
2. Credit cards
3. Home loans
4. Business accounts

743. Tele marketing means

1. Selling telephones
2. Sending SMS messages
3. Chatting on the phone
4. Marketing through phone calls

744. KYC means

1. Keep your customers cool
2. Keep your credit card
3. Know your customer
4. Know your credits

745. Digital marketing is the same as

1. Online marketing
2. Cross selling
3. Website designing
4. Road shows

746. The modern marketing concept asserts that 'marketing' starts with the product idea and ends with :

1. Production of Quality product
2. Advertisement Campaign
3. Customer Satisfaction
4. Sale of the Product

747. List of people who do not wish to receive telemarketing call is :

1. Dare Not Call List
2. **Do Not Call List**
3. Do Not Dial List
4. Do Never Call List

748. Internet Banking can be popularized by way of :

1. Reduced prices
2. Wide area network
3. Better technology
4. **More ATMs**

749. Online Marketing is the function of which of the following ?

1. Purchase section
2. Production department
3. **IT department**
4. A collective function of all stall

750. In modern day marketing, the benefits of selling extend to ……..

1. **Only products and service**
2. Only after sales services
3. Lifelong relationship with buyer
4. All of above

751. Web marketing involves

1. Selling web cameras
2. **Web advertisements**
3. e-mail chatting
4. Browsing the web

752. Online marketing is mostly useful for marketing of

1. Saving accounts

2. Credit cards
3. Home loans
4. NRI deposits

753. A call in marketing means

    1. To phone the customers
    2. To visit the customers
    3. To visit the marketing site
    4. To call on prospective customer

754. Global marketing is a result of

    1. Domestic charge
    2. Globalization
    3. Privatization
    4. All of these

755. Service marketing involves –

    1. Transaction marketing
    2. Internal marketing
    3. Relationship marketing
    4. All of these

756. Marketing of services is resorted to in –

    1. Manufacturing concerns
    2. Hotels
    3. Airlines business
    4. Only (b) and (c)

757. Internet Banking means

    1. Marketing on the net
    2. Surfing on the net
    3. Phishing

4. **Banking on the net**

758. Marketing of internet banking can be focused among –

   1. **All existing customers**
   2. All corporate
   3. All outsourced agencies
   4. All NRIs

759. Good customer service helps to boost

   1. Customer retention
   2. Better image
   3. Consumer loyalty
   4. **All of these**

760. Modern style of marketing include ……… find the wrong answer.

   1. Digital marketing
   2. Tele-marketing
   3. **Door to door marketing**
   4. e-mail solicitation

761. Online marketing is useful for

   1. **Selling old products**
   2. Sending e-mails
   3. Increased production
   4. Increased job production

762. Service marketing the same as

   1. **Internet marketing**
   2. Telemarketing
   3. Relationship marketing
   4. Marketing done by service class employees

763. "Push" marketing style requires –

   1. Proper planning
   2. Good pushing strength
   3. Ability to identify the products
   4. Aggressive marketing

764. Diversification in marketing means

   1. Marketing to different countries
   2. Marketing in many companies
   3. Marketing of the same product by many diverse persons
   4. Marketing of new diverse product

765. Modern methods of marketing include

   1. Publicity on the net
   2. Advertisement on the net
   3. Soliciting business through e-mails
   4. All of these

766. A call in marketing means –

   1. To phone the customers
   2. To visit the customers
   3. To visit the marketing site
   4. To call on prospective customer

767. What is the full form of ECB ?

   1. Extra commercial banking
   2. Extra commercial borrowing
   3. External commercial borrowing
   4. All of these

768. Global marketing is a result of

    1. Domestic charge
    2. Globalization
    3. Privatization
    4. All of these

769. .... is an example of tele-conferencing ?

    1. Computer conferencing
    2. Audio conferencing
    3. Video conferencing
    4. All of above

770. Which among the following is a disadvantage of an EDI system ?

    1. Speed
    2. Errors
    3. Expensive
    4. Mismatch

771. Traditional marketing style involves

    1. Telemarketing
    2. Digital marketing
    3. Indirect marketing
    4. Direct marketing

772. Modern marketing includes

    1. Publicity on internet
    2. Advertisement on internet
    3. Bulk e-mails
    4. All of these

773. True marketing requires

　　　1.　Command and order mindset
　　　2.　Control mindset
　　　3.　Active mindset
　　　4.　Passive mindset

774. Digital banking means

　　　1.　Banking with calculators
　　　2.　Banking with digital instruments
　　　3.　Internet banking and tele - banking
　　　4.　Export finance

775. Digital marketing means –

　　　1.　Selling by using calculators
　　　2.　Marketing of digital instruments
　　　3.　Marketing by using internet and telephones
　　　4.　Export finance

776. Customer database means

　　　1.　Customers biodata
　　　2.　Customer loyalty
　　　3.　Customers loans details
　　　4.　Information about customers needs

777. Transaction marketing means

　　　1.　Marketing only to strangers
　　　2.　Mere selling of goods
　　　3.　Doing banking transactions
　　　4.　All of the above

778. e-marketing is same as –

1. Virtual marketing
2. Digital marketing
3. Real time marketing
4. All of these

779. Digital marketing is selling –

1. Digital goods
2. Calculators
3. Through internet
4. None of these

780. Internet marketing means –

1. Internet marketing
2. Marketing to a core group
3. Marketing to employess
4. None of these

781. Internal marketing means –

1. Marketing to family members
2. Marketing to staff members
3. Marketing inside India
4. Marketing beyond India

782. Modern marketing is –

1. Telemarketing
2. Web marketing
3. Internet advertisement
4. All of these

783. Modern marketing includes –

1. Be communicated to site visitors and in all marketing communications

2. Be a clear differentiator from online competitors
3. Target market segment that the proposition will appeal to
4. **All of the above**

784. Achieving marketing objectives through use of electronic communications technology is –

1. E-marketing
2. **E-business**
3. Internet marketing
4. E-commerce

785. Using the internet for marketing research to find out customers needs is –

1. Satisfying customer requirements
2. Anticipating customer requirements
3. **Identifying customer requirements**
4. All of above

786. Assessing the demand for digital service or online revenue contribution is –

1. Anticipating customer requirements
2. Satisfying customer requirements
3. **Identifying customer requirements**
4. Ignoring customer requirements

787. Delivering e-mail based customer support is –

1. Identifying customer requirements
2. Anticipating customer requirements
3. **Satisfying customer requirements**
4. All of above

788. E-marketing plan has –

    1. Same objective as financial plans
    2. Same objectives as the marketing plan
    3. Same objectives as the e-business plan
    4. Objectives which support organizational plan

789. Direct online contribution effective is the–

    1. Reach of audience volume of a site
    2. Proportion of sales influenced by the web site
    3. Proportion of business turnover achieved by e-commerce transactions
    4. First and third option above

790. .... is not an element of a company's external micro-environment that need to be assessed during situation analysis for e-marketing ?

    1. Supplier analysis
    2. Competitor analysis
    3. Intermediary analysis
    4. Demand analysis

791. Modern marketing EXCLUDES –

    1. Digital marketing
    2. Tele – marketing
    3. Door-to-door marketing
    4. None of these

792. Online marketing is appropriate for –

    1. Selling obsolete products
    2. Sending e-mails
    3. Higher production
    4. Additional job opportunities

793. Service marketing is the same as –

   1. Internet marketing
   2. Telemarketing
   3. Internal marketing
   4. Relationship marketing

794. Modern marketing includes –

   1. Digital marketing
   2. Tele marketing
   3. E-commerce
   4. E-mails solicitation

795. E marketing is same as –

   1. Virtual marketing
   2. Digital marketing
   3. Read time marketing
   4. All of the above

796. Direct marketing is more useful when

   1. Absolute margins are very large
   2. Absolute margins are very low
   3. Absolute margins are very low
   4. Production cost is very low

797. Which of the following is not associated with a role in a buying decision making unit ?

   1. Supplier
   2. Gatekeeper
   3. Decision making
   4. Buyer

798. Which is the element of psychology of consumer ?

1. Knowledge of the customer
2. Intention
3. Attitudes
4. **All of above**

799. Which is the maturity product of a bank ?

1. Fixed term deposit
2. Senior citizen deposit scheme
3. House loan
4. **All of above**

800. Which of the following is prestige product of a bank ?

1. International debit and credit card
2. Credit card
3. ATM card
4. **All of above**

801. Who among the following is not a part of the marketing mix ?

1. Wholesalers
2. Retailers
3. **Customers**
4. All of these

802. Which of the following is the crux of marketing process ?

1. Marketing planning
2. **Marketing mix**
3. Marketing expansion
4. Market scanning

803. Which of the following comes under the decisions concerning the products ?

1. Product attributes

2. Branding and packaging
3. Product mix
4. **All of above**

804. A product is reffered to as

1. Tangible and intangibly item
2. Tangible item
3. Anything
4. **All of above**

805. A product represents a market's offering as it is perceived by

1. Present customers
2. **Potential customers**
3. Company
4. All of above

806. Which of the following information forms available to the marketing manager can usually be accessed more quickly and cheaply than other information sources?

1. Marketing intelligence
2. Marketing research
3. Customer profiles
4. **Internal databases**

807. All of the following are considered to be draw backs of local marketing EXCEPT ?

1. It can drive up manufacturing and marketing costs by reducing economies of scale
2. It can create logistical problems when the company tries to meet varied requirements
3. **It can attract unwanted competition**
4. It can dilute the brand overall image

808. That the company that overlooks new and better ways to do things will eventually lose customers to another company that has found a better way of serving customer needs is a major tenet of :

      1. **Innovative marketing**
      2. Consumer oriented marketing
      3. Value marketing
      4. Sense of mission marketing

809. Setting call objectives is done during which of the following in stages of the selling process ?

      1. Prospecting
      2. **Preapproach**
      3. Approach
      4. Handing objections

810. ………… arc products bought by individuals and organizations for further processing or for use in conducting a business.

      1. Consumer products
      2. Services
      3. **Industrial products**
      4. Specialty products

811. Customer relationship management is managing company's interaction with

      1. **Current and future customers**
      2. Sales team
      3. Services team
      4. Direct selling associations

812. The one which is not involved in the growth strategy of a company is

1. Horizontal integration
2. Diversification
3. Intensification
4. **None of these**

813. What does lead generation mean ?

 1. **Likely source for prospective clients**
 2. Tips for selling tactics
 3. Tips for better production
 4. Motivating the sales force

814. An efficient marketing style does not require which of the following ?

 1. Teamwork
 2. Proper planning
 3. Good communication skills
 4. **None of above**

815. Which of the following is not a part of the modern style of marketing ?

 1. Digital marketing
 2. Tele-marketing
 3. e-mail solicitation
 4. **none of these**

816. What do you mean by customization?

 1. **Special products to suit each customer**
 2. Acquiring more customers
 3. New innovative products
 4. More products per customer

817. In terms of banking industry, what does ROA stand for ?

1. Rate of allocation
2. Ratio of assets
3. **Return on assets**
4. Return on advances

818. Marketing can be best defined as

   1. To focus only on products or services
   2. Meeting human needs profitably
   3. To focus on customers
   4. **Only (b) and (c)**

819. Identify the only correct statement among the following.

   1. Marketing is a waste of employees' time
   2. Marketing is not required in India due to its vast population
   3. Only marketing involves extra work
   4. **Marketing includes promotion, sellin, research and advertising**

820. What does market information mean ?

   1. **Knowledge of customer profile and product mix**
   2. Knowledge of shopping malls and super markets
   3. Knowledge of small shops and street markets
   4. Knowledge of various languages

821. Leads can be best sourced from

   1. Foreign customers
   2. Yellow pages
   3. List of vendors
   4. **Local supply chains**

822. A successful marketing person requires one of the following qualities :

1. **Empathy**
2. Sympathy
3. Insistence
4. Aggressiveness

823. Innovation in marketing is the same as

1. Communication
2. **Creativity**
3. Aspiration
4. Research work

824. Market segmentation can be resorted to by dividing the target group as per

1. **Income levels of customers**
2. Needs of the salespersons
3. Marketing skill of the employees
4. Size of the organization

825. Post-sales activities include

1. **Customer's feedback**
2. Customer identification
3. Customer's apathy
4. Product design

826. The competitive position of a company can be improved by

1. Increasing the selling price
2. Reducing the margin
3. Ignoring competitors
4. **Understanding and fulfilling customers needs**

827. A good brand can be built up by way of

1. Customer grievances

2. Break down of IT support
3. Large number of products
4. **Consistent offering of good services**

828. Buying and selling in the marketing functions are categorized as

1. Distribution functions
2. Facilitating functions
3. **Exchange function**
4. All of above

829. Which among the following is the most basic concept underlying marketing ?

1. Marketing
2. Product
3. **Needs, want and demands**
4. All of above

830. The need or want of a particular product becomes a demand, when

1. **It is backed by buying power**
2. The product service is available
3. A product represents that particular need
4. All of these

831. Which among the following is called life blood of business ?

1. Product
2. Marketing
3. **Finance**
4. All of above

832. Which among the following is included in marketing decisions ?

1. Project cost decision
2. **Promotion decision**
3. Finance decision
4. All of above

833. Which among the following is a customer oriented concept ?

1. Production concept
2. **Marketing concept**
3. Selling concept
4. All of above

834. If marketing is done effectively which of the following is not required ?

1. **Publicity**
2. Advertisement
3. Market research
4. Market segmentation

835. Marketing information means

1. Knowledge of shopping malls
2. Knowledge of customers profile and product mix
3. Knowledge of various languages
4. **Knowledge of shops and bazaars**

836. To investigate new markets .... management function is important.

1. Finance functions
2. **Marketing**
3. Production
4. HRM

837. Companies selling mass consumer goods and services such as soft drinks, cosmetics, air travel and athletic shoes and

equipment spend a great deal of time trying to establish a superior brand image in markets called –

1. Business markets
2. Global markets
3. **Consumer markets**
4. Service markets

838. In relationship marketing firms focus on .... relationships with ....

1. Short term; customers and suppliers
2. **Long term; customers and suppliers**
3. Short term; customers
4. Long term; customers

839. Which of the following statements is correct ?

1. Marketing is the term used to refer only to the sales function within a firm
2. Marketing managers don't usually get involved in production or distribution decisions
3. Marketing is an activity that considers only the needs of the organization; not the needs of society as a whole.
4. **Marketing is the activity, set of institutions, and processes for creating, communicating, delivering, and exchanging offerings that have value for customers, clients, partners, and society at large**

840. Buying and selling of mass consumer goods and services comes under which of the following markets ?

1. Business markets
2. Global markets
3. **Consumer markets**
4. Government markets

841. Which of the following is a set of promises that the brand makes to customers ?

    1. Brand contract
    2. Brand association
    3. Brand persona
    4. Brand equity

842. Which of the following is not a method of promotion ?

    1. Advertising
    2. Retailing
    3. Direct mail
    4. Public relations

843. A business wishes to reach a wide audience who would otherwise not know about its product. Which method of promotion is likely to be most effective at achieving this ?

    1. Direct mail
    2. Email
    3. Advertising
    4. Sponsorship
    5. None of these

844. If lots of customers like the brand and are inclined to be bound into a contract, they would be known as

    1. Loyal customer
    2. Difficult customer
    3. Potential customer
    4. Finicky customer

845. Positioning has to stem from the point of view of –

    1. Customers
    2. Competitors
    3. General managers
    4. Brand owners

846. .... determines why customers buy?

 1. **Customer needs analysis**
 2. Brand based customer model
 3. Good pushing strength
 4. Brand management process

847. 'Push' marketing style requires –

 1. Proper planning
 2. Good pushing strength
 3. Ability to identify products
 4. **Aggressive marketing**

848. The three step process within marketing segmentation includes :

 1. Segmentation, Targeting and Positioning
 2. Targeting, Segmentation, and Positioning
 3. **Segmentation, Targeting and Positioning**
 4. Positioning, Mass Marketing and Segmentation

849. Which of the following is not a commonly-used age segment ?

 1. Retires
 2. Generation X
 3. **Achievers**
 4. Baby boomers

850. In positioning statement, the first thing that must be stated is

 1. **Target segment**
 2. Market segmentation
 3. Differentiation
 4. Positioning

851. The positioning statement first states the

   1. **Product membership in category**
   2. Points of priority
   3. Points of differences
   4. Brands superiority

852. The process in which firm tries to expand the market for mature brand by focusing on number of brand users and usage rate user is known as

   1. **Market modification**
   2. Product modification
   3. Marketing program modification
   4. Market segmentation

853. A short term loan is repayable within –

   1. 20 years
   2. **3 years**
   3. As per the borrowers' wish
   4. There is no need to repay short term loans

854. Internet banking can be popularized by way of :

   1. Higher prices
   2. Wide area network
   3. Better technology
   4. **More ATMs**

855. Difference between direct and indirect bank marketing is

   1. Direct marketing is to outsiders, indirect is to employees
   2. Direct marketing is to bank's owners indirect is to outsiders
   3. Direct marketing is to other bank's employees. Indirect is to outsiders
   4. **None of these**

856. Which among the following is the main advantage of depth interviews ?

    1. Accurate information
    2. Hidden information
    3. Time saving
    4. High cost

857. What do you mean by Delphi Technique in Market Research ?

    1. In this a questionnaire is prepared
    2. Depth interviews are conducted
    3. Information is elicited by means of discussions with various experts in the field
    4. All of above

858. For routinely purchased items, buyers are frequently the :

    1. Users
    2. Influencers
    3. Deciders
    4. Gatekeepers
    5.

859. The demand for many industrial products for which a price increase or decrease will not significantly affect the demand is

    1. Elastic
    2. Inelastic
    3. Derived
    4. Joint

860. In modern days sales approach is based on

    1. Value sharing
    2. Relation building

3. Co-ordinated approach
4. **All the above**

861. M-Commerce is a new term in latest marketing technique. It is

1. **Misuse of mobile phones and E-commerce**
2. Mobile phones in marketing
3. Marketing by commerce students
4. Mega commercial activities

862. What is the first thing about an advertisement that attracts our attention ?

1. **Product**
2. Music
3. Model
4. Special effects

863. The nature of internet commerce can best be described as

1. **Tangible**
2. None-territorial
3. Territorial
4. Both (a) and (b)

864. The law of pull and push of web marketing refers to

1. **Pull people to your site, then push quality information to them**
2. Pull people to your site and force them to purchase
3. Push people into your business
4. Pull the interest of people

865. As a counselor, a personnel manager

1. Reminds the management of moral obligations towards employees

2. Encourages the employees
3. Tries to settle the disputes between labour and management
4. All of the above

867. If the market share of a company is increasing

1. **It is a sign progress**
2. The company must take action to arrest the trend
3. Both (a) and (b)
4. Neither (a) nor (b)

868. 'Benchmark' means ?

1. Products lined up on a bench
2. Salesman sitting on a bench
3. **Set standards**
4. Mark on a bench

869. Bank assurance means ?

1. Assurance given by banks to loaners
2. Assurance to bank with one bank
3. Assurance to give good service
4. **Selling insurance product through banks**

870. Consumer behavior perception is a process through which

1. A consumer make ultimate purchasing
2. A consumer is satisfied
3. **A consumer's mind receives organizes and interprets physical stimuli**
4. Both (a) and (c)

871. In case of diamond, if the price goes up slightly, demand will fall by a much larger margin. The demand is

1. Zero elastic
2. **Highly price elastic**
3. Income elastic
4. Low price elastic

872. I he purchase to ………. is least likely to be altected by demographic factors

1. **Table salt**
2. A computer for home use
3. Fast food
4. Low fat cheese

873. Advertising creates consumers demand for products that they would otherwise not feel need to buy. This statement is

1. **Partially true**
2. Absolutely true
3. Partially biased
4. All of these

874. Which among the following is a fundamental right of consumer ?

1. Right to safety
2. Right to be informed
3. Right to choose
4. **All the above**

875. …………. Includes practices such as overstating the product's features or performance, during the customer to the store for a bargain that is out of stock, or running rigged contests.

1. **Deceptive promotion**
2. Deceptive packaging
3. Deceptive pricing
4. Deceptive cost structure

876. Sales targets are fixed on the basis of

    1. Past experience
    2. Time period
    3. Brand positionary
    4. All the above

877. Marketers should view packaging as a major strategic tool, especially for

    1. Consumer convenience products
    2. Consumer shopping products
    3. Industrial products
    4. Specialty products

878. A true marketing requires

    1. Command and other mindset
    2. Control mindset
    3. Passive mindset
    4. Active mindset

879. The label on a soft drink reads "cool and refreshing". For what reason are these words used ?

    1. To provide information
    2. To encourage multiple purchases
    3. To promote the product
    4. To satisfy legal requirements

880. One distinguishing factor between a brand name and a brand mark is that a brand name

    1. Creates customer loyalty
    2. Consists of words
    3. Identifies only one item in the product mix
    4. Implies an organization name

881. The four levels of brands are the tangible product, the basic brand the potential brand and the _____ brand

   1. Targeted
   2. **Augmented**
   3. Aggregated
   4. Positioned

882. Which of the following sentences is true ?

   1. Marketing is not required in a Buyer's market
   2. **Marketing is not required in a seller's market**
   3. Marketing is not required due to competition
   4. Marketing is not required due to globalization

883. For effective marketing the salesman should have which of these qualities

   1. Team spirit
   2. Motivation
   3. Effective communication skills
   4. **All of these**

884. Consumer of a bank comes under which of the following environment ?

   1. Internal environment
   2. **External environment**
   3. Indirect environment
   4. All of these

885. labeling is important for three reasons, including promotional and legal reasons. What is the third reason ?

   1. Marketing
   2. Branding
   3. Strategic
   4. **Informational**

886. Which among the following is / are advantages of packaging ?

   1. It helps increase sales
   2. It adds to the use of product
   3. It help in storage
   4. All of above

887. A brand manager in a multiproduct firm would be considered responsible for

   1. The performance of a specific brand
   2. All brands within a product line
   3. Branding the products of the firm
   4. All brands made by the firm

888. All of the following are major in developing new products except

   1. Test marketing
   2. Evaluation of competitors efforts
   3. Screening
   4. Idea generation

889. Aggressive pricing is typical during the stage of the product life cycle

   1. Decline
   2. Growth
   3. Introduction
   4. Stabilization

890. A product mix is best described as

   1. All products offered by a firm
   2. Product distribution promotion and price
   3. All products of a particular type
   4. A group of closely related products

891. What does the acronym FMCG refer to ?

   1. Functional / mid-riced, or compulsory goods
   2. Famous, manufacturer's clothing goods
   3. Fast moving consumer goods
   4. Frequent market consumption goods

892. A prospect means ?

   1. Any customer who walks into the bank
   2. A customer who is likely to be interested in bank's product or service
   3. A depositor of the bank
   4. A borrower of the bank

893. The real value of marketing research to the organization can best be understood by

   1. Its immediate impact on profits
   2. The amount of time spent
   3. How much it costs
   4. Improvements in the ability to make decisions

894. The first step in planning a marketing research project is :

   1. Conducting a cost / benefit analysis
   2. Searching the environment
   3. Defining and locating problems
   4. Assessing organization resources

895. The major Disadvantage of a mail survey versus a telephone or personal interview survey is

   1. Having to offer incentives
   2. The low response rate
   3. The elimination of interview bias
   4. Cost

896. The XKL company wants to adopt the marketing concept. To be consistent with this move, it should adopt which of the following philosophies ?

       1.   **The customer is always right**
       2.   Making money is our business
       3.   Sell, sell, sell
       4.   Keep price low

897. Boldnew, the maker of a highly innovative light bulb, finds that it has excess stocks. The firm increases its advertising budget by 50 per cent and doubles its sales staff. This company is operating as if it were operating

       1.   Production
       2.   **Sales**
       3.   Marketing
       4.   Social

898. Chrysler's Chief Executive Officer is the company's spokesperson. His message has focused on concern for customers and product quality. Which aspect of implementing the marketing concept does this represent ?

       1.   Focusing on general conditions
       2.   Stressing the short run
       3.   **Endorsement of the marketing concept by top management**
       4.   Development of an information system

899. Which of the following is an example of a problem that may arise in the implementation of the marketing concept ?

       1.   **By satisfying one segment in society, a firm contributes to the dissatisfaction of other segments**
       2.   Consumers do not understand what the marketing concept is

3. Dealers do not support the marketing concept
4. A product may fit the needs of too many segments

900. Most specifically, marketing strategy :

1. Is concerned with key decisions required to reach an objective
2. **Encompasses selecting and analyzing a target market and creating and maintaining an appropriate marketing mix**
3. Expands geographic boundaries of markets to serve larger geographic areas
4. Involves determining the direction and objectives of marketing management

901. All of the following are marketing management tasks EXCEPT :

1. Marketing planning
2. Organizing marketing activities
3. Co-ordinating marketing activities
4. **Project development and analysis**

902. Management is the compulsory process of –

1. **Decision Making**
2. Lapse
3. Final Decision
4. Interim Decision

903. Which of the following is the most important responsibility of a manager ?

1. Allowing Fraud
2. Making Product
3. **Taking Decision**
4. Withdrawing Salary

904. Who said – "Decision making is the selection based on some material from two or more posses alternative" ?

    1. **George R. Terry**
    2. Earnest Dale
    3. Philip Kotler
    4. Koontz & O'Donnel

905. Who said – "Decision is the relection from among alternatives of a course of actions" ?

    1. Marshal
    2. **Koontz & O'Donnel**
    3. Earnest Dale
    4. Pankaj Parashar
    5. Dr. Manmohan Singh

906. **Statement(I):** A form of non- store retailing that uses advertising to contact consumers who, in turn, purchase products without visiting a retail store is called Direct selling.

    Statement(II): A form of non-store retailing in which personal contact between a sales person and a consumer occurs away from a retail store is called Direct Marketing.

In the light of above statements, identify the correct code of statements being correct or incorrect.

a. Statement (I) is correct but Statement (II) is not correct.
b. Statement (I) is not correct but Statement (II) is correct.
c. Both the statements are correct.
d. Both the statements are not correct.

907. 34% of the customers who fall in one of the categories of diffusion process who are deliberate customers to accept an innovation just before the average adopter in a social system. Such customers who are above average in social and economic measures, rely quite a bit on advertisements and salesmen are known as:

    a. Early Adopters   **b. Early Majority**   c. Late Majority   d. Late Adopters

908. The G. E. Business Model is explained on which one of the following parameters?

a. **Market Attractiveness and Business Position.**

b. Business Attractiveness and Market Position.

c. Industry Growth rate and Company's Market share.

d. Company's Growth rate and Industry's Position.

909. A reduction from the list price that is offered by a seller to buyers in payment for marketing functions the buyers will perform is

a. Trade Discount b. Functional Discount

c. Cash Discount d. **Both Trade and Functional Discount**

known as:

910. A research technique used particularly in retailing (online and offline), in which consumers are recruited by researchers to act as anonymous buyers in order to evaluate customer satisfaction, service quality and customer's own evaluation of their experiences, is known as :

a. Consumer Jury b. Projective Technique

c. **Mystery Shopping** d. Semiotic Research

911. Which of the following is not a measure for quality of service for consumer ?

a. Responsiveness
b. Competition
c. Empathy
d. Tangibility

912. Which of the following is a targeting strategy ?

a. Standardization
b. Differentiation
c. Focus
d. All of the above

913. Match the items of List-I with items of List-II and indicate the code of correct matching.

List - I **List - II**
A. Real Needs i. Expecting good service from car dealer.
B. Unstated Needs ii. Customer expects to be seen by his friends as value-oriented savvy consumer.
C. Delight Needs iii. Customer wants car at low operational cost and not initial cost.
D. Secret Needs iv. Customer receives free insurance on purchase of car.

Codes :

	A	B	C	D
a.	iii	i	iv	ii
b.	i	iii	ii	iv
c.	ii	iv	I	iii
d.	iv	ii	I	iii

914. **Statement I :** The firm should "stick to its niching" but not necessarily to its niche.

Statement II : Multiple niching is not preferable to single niching.

Codes :
   a. Both the Statements are true.
   b. Both the Statements are false.
   c. Statement I is true, but Statement II is false.
   d. Statement II is true, but Statement I is false.

915. A descriptive thought that a person holds about something is called

   a. Belief
   b. Learning
   c. Attitude
   d. Perception

916. The concept of achieving maximum profits through increased consumer satisfaction for raised market share focuses on

a. Product
b. Selling
c. Customer
d. Production

916. Match the following items of List-I (sources of competition) with List-II (examples for these sources of competition) and indicate the code of correct matching.

List – I

a. Directly similar products
b. Available substitutes
c. Unrelated products

List - II
  i. OLA Taxi and Metro Rail
 ii. Mercedes and BMW
iii. PVR and Amusement park

Codes :
(A) (B) (C)

a.	iii	ii	i
b.	i	iii	ii
c.	i	ii	iii
d.	**ii**	**i**	**iii**

917. The marketing task which finds ways to alter the time pattern of demand through flexible pricing, promotion and other incentives is called

      a.   Demarketing
      b.   **Synchromarketing**
      c.   Fleximarketing
      d.   Gorilla Marketing

918. Which of the following is not a reason for a firm to lose its market share to competitors?

a. **A product/model is perceived by the target customer group as satisfying needs.**
b. Customers not being covered by the company's sales force and distribution outlets.
c. Customers may have been lost to competitors due to poor service by the firm or its sales personnel or product becoming obsolete or more expensive.
d. All the above are correct reasons for given condition.

919. Match the items of List-I with List-II and denote the code of correct matching.

List - I

a. Invest Strategy
b. Protect Strategy
c. Harvest Strategy
d. Divest Strategy

List – II

i. No receiving of new resources.

ii. Well financed marketing efforts.
iii. Selective resource allocation
iv. Not warranting substantial new resources.

Codes :

	A	B	C	D
a.	**ii**	**iii**	**iv**	**i**
b.	i	iii	ii	iv
c.	ii	i	iv	iii
d.	iv	iii	ii	i

920. An elaborated version of the idea expressed in meaningful consumer term is called

a. Product image
b. Product idea
c. Product concept
d. Prototype

921. Which of the following requires consumers to interpret ambiguous stimuli?

a. Focus group method
b. Projective techniques
c. Rejective techniques
d. Semantic differential scales

922. Which of the following passes through the four stages of distinctiveness, emulation, mass fashion and decline ?

1. Style
2. Fashion
3. Fad
4. Style and Fashion

923. Which of the following positioning strategies is adopted by marketers to position their product in two categories simultaneously ?

1. Point of Difference

2. Point of Parity
3. **Straddle Positioning**
4. Emotional Positioning

924. **Statement (I)** : Marketing is the process by which a firm profitably translates customer needs into revenue.
Statement (II) : Marketing is the messages and/or actions that causes messages and/or actions.
Codes :
1. (I) is correct but (II) is not correct.
2. (II) is correct but (I) is not correct.
3. **(I) and (II) both are correct.**
4. (I) and (II) both are incorrect.

925. **Assertion (A)** : Odd pricing aims at maximising profit by making micro-adjustments in pricing structure.
Reasoning (R) : Odd pricing refers to a price ending in 1, 3, 5, 7, or 9. When examining a price, the first digits carry more weight than the last ones.
Codes :
1. (A) is right and (R) is wrong.
2. (A) is wrong and (R) is right.
3. **Both (A) and (R) are right.**
4. Both (A) and (R) are wrong.

926. Name the process in which a buyer posts its interest in buying a certain quantity of item and sellers compete for the business by submitting lower bid until there is only one seller left.

a. Internet
b. **Reverse auction**
c. B2B market place
d. B2C market place

927. Advertising method in which an advertisement is broadcasted simultaneously on several radio stations and / or television channels is known as

a. Black-out

b. Consolidation
c. **Road-block**
d. Cornering

928. Which type of differentiation is used to gain competitive advantage through the way a firm designs its distribution coverage, expertise and performance ?

a. **Channel differentiation**
b. Services differentiation
c. People differentiation
d. Product   differentiation

929. Which one of the following is the most likely result of a marketing strategy that attempts to serve all potential customers ?
      5. All customers will be delighted.
      6. Customer-perceived value will be increased.
      7. The company will need to follow up with a demarketing campaign.
      8. **Not all customers will be satisfied.**

930. Which of the following is not a primary activity in Michael Porter's value chain ?

a. Inbound logistics
b. Operations
c. Outbound logistics
d. **Procurement**

931. Which of the following represents consistency of results when the test instrument is used repeatedly ?

a. Validity
b. **Reliability**
c. Relativity
d. Sensitivity

932. **Assertion (A) :** Too many stimuli make a person accommodated to those sensations. Sensory adaptation is a problem that concerns

many advertisers, which is why they try to change their advertising campaigns regularly.

Reason (R) : To cut through advertising clutter and to ensure that consumers perceive advertisement, marketers try to increase sensory input.

Codes :

    a. (A) is right and (R) is wrong.
    b. (A) is wrong and (R) is right.
    c. Both (A) and (R) are right but (R) does not explain (A).
    d. Both (A) and (R) are right and (R) explains (A).

933. Who said "If the buyer in a transaction is buying for purposes of re-sale or to further his business operations, the seller in that same transaction is engaged in whole saling" ?

    1. Philip Kotler
    2. Cundiff and Still
    3. Dr. Diya Parashar
    4. William J. Stanton

934. These type of goods are always purchased by wholesalers –

    1. Inferior
    2. Superior
    3. Huge Quantity
    4. Durable

935. Basically merchant wholesalrs who do not provide full services, and often provide only the minimum services is known as

    1. General Merchanise wholesaler
    2. General live wholesaler
    3. Speciality wholesaler
    4. Limited Function wholesaler

936. Wholesalers make proper balance in between –

   1. Costs and profit
   2. Demand and supply
   3. Buyer and seller
   4. Government and Producer

937. Which is not an example of Large Scale Trading ?

   1. Speciality Shop
   2. Departmental store
   3. Super Bazar
   4. Shopping Malls

938. 'Bata showroom' is an example of –

   1. Departmental stores
   2. Multiple shops
   3. Co-operative societies
   4. All of above

939. A Restaurant may be a part of –

   1. Departmental store
   2. Super Bazar
   3. Multiple shops
   4. 1 & 2
   5. 2 & 3

940. The name of distribution channel which is run by producers directly is known as

   1. Departmental store
   2. Multiple shops
   3. Hire purchase shops
   4. MOB
   5. Small shops

941. Which business organization requires more and effective advertisement support among the following ?

    1. Departmental store
    2. Supper Bazar
    3. Multiple store
    4. MOB
    5. Ration shops

942. Among the following which business organization have the widest scope ?

    1. Departmental store
    2. Super Bazar
    3. Chain shops
    4. Mail order business Houses
    5. Ration shops

943. What is the advantage of advertisement society has ?

    1. Employment opportunity
    2. Increase in standard of living
    3. Encouragement to healthy competition
    4. Education
    5. All of above

944. Name the advantage of advertisement under which it provides complete information about the product to the society :

    1. Utilization
    2. Fuller utilization
    3. Educative
    4. Help
    5. Stress

945. Advertisement provides knowledge of new products and commodities to the society to

1. Increase in sale
2. Increase in fraud
3. **Increase in standard of living**
4. Help
5. Education

946. Newspapers are sold for very cheaper rates because

1. It contains discount coupon
2. It is used for criminal activities
3. **It contains advertisement**
4. It enjoys subsidy
5. All of the above

947. Through advertisement consumers used to take their purchasing decision in advance. In this way advertisement helps in

1. **Convenient purchasing**
2. Purchasing parity
3. Purchasing parity
4. Purchase return
5. Social obligation
6. After purchase / sale service

948. Which advertisement media will you prefer to market the product at national level ?

1. Loca news papers
2. **Television**
3. Wall painting
4. Posters
5. Periodicels

949. Which advertisement media will you prefer for immediate effect of it ?

1. News paper
2. Periodicels

3. Radio
4. Posters
5. **1, 3 & 4**

950. Collective bargaining is a main characteristic of –

1. Super bazaar
2. Chained shops
3. **Co-operative societies**
4. Departmental store
5. None of these

951. Retailing is defined as all the activities involved in selling goods or services directly to final consumer for –

1. Black marketing
2. Personal use
3. Business use
4. **Personal and business use**
5. None of these

952. Retailing is defined as all the activities involved in selling goods and services directly to find consumer for personal and business use.

1. True in large scale trade
2. Trade in PSU's
3. True in emergency
4. True
5. **False**

953. Super markets are large low costs high margin high volume self stores that carry a wide range of food. Laundry and Household products.

1. False for small towns
2. True
3. True in case of rural area

4. **False**
5. Can't say

954. Retailers must decide on three product variables- product assortment, services, mix and price.

1. True
2. True in the some cases
3. True in special cases
4. **False**
5. False in some Geographical areas

955. Which of the following is not a service level offered by retailers ?

1. Limited service
2. Self service
3. **Quality service**
4. Full service
5. Quality service

956. Which is not a type of Retailer ?

1. Doctor's seeing patient
2. Real estate agents
3. Wedworths safety
4. Avon
5. **Avon representatives**

957. Convenience stores must charge high price to make up for higher operating costs and lower   sales volume.

1. **True**
2. True up to some extent
3. False
4. True in some special conditions
5. False when one products is purchased

958. Alteration, complaints handling and delivery are a few examples of primary services that a full service retailer should offer.

 1. **True**
 2. False
 3. True there is no showroom
 4. True when these is monopoly in the market
 5. False when consumer court exist

959. Which of the following is the best definitions of chain shops ?

 1. A group of consumers who band together to get and volume pricing from manufactures
 2. A group of volunteers who shop for handicap individual
 3. Retailers that volunteer to carry new, united products
 4. **Independently owned retailers who are sponsored by a wholesaler to engage in bulk buying and common merchandising**
 5. None of above

960. Which of the following stores has high gross margin, narrow product assortment and high level of service ?

 1. Convenience store
 2. Supermarkets
 3. **Speciality stores**
 4. Departmental stores
 5. Ration shops

961. Wholesaling includes all the activities involved in selling goods and services to these buying for resale or business use.

 1. True in case of big wholesalers
 2. True in case of registered wholesalers
 3. True in case of Indian wholesalers
 4. **True**
 5. False in case of producer retailer

962. An agent is wholesalers who does not take title to goods and whose function is to bring   buyers and sallers together and assist in negotiation

    1. False
    2. False in case of single wholesalers
    3. True
    4. True when reserve price applicable
    5. True agent is a wholesalers as well as retailer

963. Traditional / normal store retailers face increasing competition from which of the following   new store retailers ?

    1. Print catalogues
    2. Print cartons
    3. Online computer shopping service
    4. Television shopping shows
    5. 1, 3 and 4

964. A wholesaler that takes title to the merchandise they handle, is known as a –

    1. Simple wholesalers
    2. Merchant wholesalers
    3. Commission merchants
    4. Agent
    5. Brokers

965. A major trend wholeselling is that wholeselling companies will grow larger, primarily   through acquisitions, merger and geographical expansion

    1. True when only one wholesalers in market
    2. True when wholesalers has so many branches
    3. True
    4. False
    5. False when wholesalers charges different prices

966. Which of the following is not a function carried out by whole salers ?

    1. Making fraud deals
    2. Providing quicker delivery to buyers
    3. Holding inventories
    4. Financial customers buy giving credit
    5. Provide after sale service to customers

967. What is the decision that can be taken after research of products and services ?

    1. Development of production
    2. Product diversification
    3. Product simplification
    4. Changes in product
    5. All of above

968. Research which relates to entire market is called –

    1. Market research
    2. Field research
    3. Product research
    4. Taste research
    5. Attitude research

969. Which research is meant to forecast the demand of products on the basis of analysis of markets ?

    1. Research on product
    2. Research on market
    3. Research on policies
    4. Research on sales
    5. Research on consumers

970. The fields analysed under research on markets is to

    1. Study the nature of customers

2. Study the habits of customers
3. Study the tastes of customers
4. Study the attitudes of customers
5. **All of above**

971. Which of the following researches is meant to study deferent aspects of sale in an enterprises ?

6. **Research on sales methods and policies**
7. Research on sales markets and policies
8. Research on sales product and policies
9. Research on customer and policies
10. A research on sales advertisement and policies

972. The aspect which is studied in Research on sales methods and policies is –

1. **Classification of sales territories**
2. Amendments in sale territories
3. Study of competitors territories
4. Development of new sale territories
5. All of above

973. Study of the different media of advertisement is called –

1. Advertisement research
2. Product research
3. **Market research**
4. Potential research
5. Miscellaneous research

974. What type of decision affects the product line ?

1. **Major decisions**
2. Minor
3. Routine
4. Rare
5. Policy

975. Which of the following is one of the criterion of Major Decisions ?

    1.   To produce a new product or not
    2.   To continue the production of existing product
    3.   To provide the credit facility to consumers
    4.   1 and 3
    5.   **1, 2 and 3**

976. Which decision is based on careful study and analysis of relevant factors ?

    1.   **Major decisions**
    2.   Minor decisions
    3.   Routine decisions
    4.   Rare decisions
    5.   Policy decisions

977. Name the decisions which are made for the implementation of major decisions.

    1.   Policy decision
    2.   Rare decision
    3.   **Minor decision**
    4.   Major decision
    5.   Routine decision

978. Which of the following decisions affect the demand of a product ?

    1.   Routine decision
    2.   **Minor decision**
    3.   Major decision
    4.   Rare decision
    5.   Policy decision

979. Which of the following is an example of Minor decisions ?

    1. Colour of product
    2. Design of product
    3. Packing of product
    4. Form of product
    5. All of above

980. Marketing is –

    1. Consumer oriented
    2. Product oriented
    3. Marketing oriented
    4. 1 or 3
    5. 1, 2 and 3

981. Firstly business must find out what the

    1. Consumer want
    2. Market demand
    3. Product create
    4. Competitor supplies
    5. All of above

982. What is offered for sale should be determined by

    1. Consumer
    2. Market
    3. Antherities
    4. Government
    5. Competitors

983. Marketing starts and ends with –

    1. Consumer
    2. Market
    3. Product
    4. Taxes

        5.   MRP

984. What type of relation producer has with customers in older days ?

        1.   Simple
        2.   Direct
        3.   Indirect
        4.   Complex
        5.   Traditional

985. Now a days producers has .... relation with consumer

        1.   Indirect
        2.   Direct
        3.   Simple
        4.   Complex
        5.   Traditional

986. A market transaction take place when there is a successful matching of .... take place.

        1.   Product
        2.   Buyer & seller
        3.   Government
        4.   Producer
        5.   Tax Authorities

987. What is the basis on which power to influence a transaction depends ?

        1.   Muscle power
        2.   Discount
        3.   Competitive strength
        4.   Purchasing strength
        5.   Selling strength

988. Marketing should start –

1. **Before production**
2. After production
3. During production
4. As per the nature of the product
5. None of these

989. Marketing is a process because –

1. It comprises a series of Functions
2. It comprises a series of Mishandling
3. **It comprises a series of frauds**
4. It comprises a series of Mischiefs
5. It comprises a series of products

990. To whom producer is giving more attention rather than production, now a days ?

1. **Government**
2. Females
3. Consumers
4. Male members of society
5. Taxes

991. Who said- "Marketing is the business" ?

1. Peter F. Drucker
2. Philip kotler
3. Marshal
4. Robinson
5. **Clark**

992. In what ways Marketing is important to the society ?

1. Delivery of standard of living
2. Decrease in distribution cost
3. Increase in employment opportunities
4. Increase in national income
5. **All of above**

993. Marketing would have authority over –

   1. Product innovation
   2. Planning
   3. Production scheduling
   4. Sales
   5. All of above

994. As per modern scenario the concept of marketing is that goods must reach customers at maximum speed but with –

   1. Minimum quality
   2. Minimum price
   3. Maximum moisture
   4. Maximum packing
   5. Maximum spoiled condition

995. Marketing is being treated as

   1. Science & Art both
   2. Art
   3. Mathematics
   4. English

996. Marketing was born as –

   1. The step child of Economic
   2. The step child of Mathematics
   3. The step child of English
   4. The step child of Art
   5. The step child Accountancy

997. In part marketing is synonymous with

   1. Selling
   2. Product

3. Marketing
4. Market
5. Producer

998. Marketing is an art because –

1. It has body of rules
2. It has body of principles
3. **Standardization**
4. Market information
5. All of above

999. Marketing rules / principles can not be accurate as, the rules of –

1. **Science**
2. Physics
3. Chemistry
4. 1 and 3
5. 1, 2 and 3

1000. The market process involves, which functions ?

1. Buying
2. Transporting
3. Storing
4. Selling
5. Grading
6. Financing
7. Risk-bearing
8. Dividing

Codes :

1. 1, 3 and 4
2. 1, 2, 3, 6 and 7
3. Only 3
4. **All of the above**

NOTES

NOTES

NOTES

Other books by the Writers of this book
Price

1. HUMAN RESOURCE MANAGEMENT (1000 MCQ BOOK)   250/-

2. BUSINESS MANAGEMENT(1000 MCQ BOOK)   250/-

3. **BUSINESS ECONOICS(1000 MCQ BOOK)**   **250/-**

4. BANKING AND FINANCIAL INSTIUTIONS(1000 MCQ BOOK)   250/-

5. FINANICAL MANAGEMENT(1000 MCQ BOOK)   300/-

6. INTERNATIONAL BUSINESS(1000 MCQ BOOK)   250/-

7. **BUSINESS ENVIRNMENT(1000 MCQ BOOK)**   **250/-**

8. INCOME TAX LAW AND PLANNING(1000 MCQ BOOK)   350/-

9. BUSINESS STATISTICS AND DATA PROCESSING (1000 MCQ BOOK) 350/-

10. COST AND MANAGEMENT ACCOUNTING (1000 MCQ BOOK) 350/-

11. MARATHAN BOOK FOR NTA NET (20,000 MCQ BOOK) 950/-

www.ingramcontent.com/pod-product-compliance
Lightning Source LLC
Chambersburg PA
CBHW030616220526
45463CB00004B/1306